ABOUT THE AUTHOR

"I grew up as an only, but not lonely, boy on a farm near the little town of Julian in southeastern Nebraska," David F. Costello writes. "From the time I could walk, I haunted the local woods, prairies and fields the year around, watching birds, animals and insects. About the age of ten I took my violin into the woods and attempted to imitate bird calls, but with little success. At the same time I attempted to photograph wild animals with a box camera. The pictures were poor. But, as John Kieran puts it in his book, *Footnotes on Nature,* I did, indeed, love the country 'from childhood's earliest hour.'"

David Costello's love of nature grew with education, experience and research. After graduation from Nebraska State Teachers College, he obtained his M.S. in botany and geology from the University of Chicago and his Ph.D. in plant ecology from the same institution. While teaching botany for six years at Marquette University in Milwaukee, he was impelled to transmit his understanding of the out-of-doors to others through lectures, writing and photographs.

Mr. Costello spent 30 years in the research branch of the U. S. Forest Service, and ended his Forest Service career in 1965 as Chief, Division of Range, Wildlife Habitat and Recreation Research. He now works full time at outdoor writing and photography.

Mr. Costello and his wife, Cecilia, enjoy camping, and Mrs. Costello has never objected to having porcupines in the garage, pet crows in the yard, chipmunks and rabbits in the living room, ant farms in the playroom, and photographic equipment and books all over the house. The Costellos live in Portland, Oregon.

THE WORLD OF THE PORCUPINE

A LIVING WORLD BOOK
John K. Terres, Editor

LIVING WORLD BOOKS

John K. Terres, Editor

The World of the American Elk by Joe Van Wormer
The World of the Ant by David F. Costello
The World of the Beaver by Leonard Lee Rue III
The World of the Bison by Ed Park
The World of the Black Bear by Joe Van Wormer
The World of the Bobcat by Joe Van Wormer
The World of the Bottlenosed Dolphin
     by David K. Caldwell and Melba C. Caldwell
The World of the Canada Goose by Joe Van Wormer
The World of the Coyote by Joe Van Wormer
The World of the Frog and the Toad by George Porter
The World of the Gray Squirrel
     by Frederick S. Barkalow, Jr., and Monica Shorten
The World of the Great Horned Owl
     by G. Ronald Austing and John B. Holt, Jr.
The World of the Grizzly Bear by W. J. Schoonmaker
The World of the Gull by David F. Costello
The World of the Moose by Joe Van Wormer
The World of the Opossum by James F. Keefe
The World of the Otter by Ed Park
The World of the Porcupine by David F. Costello
The World of the Prairie Dog by David F. Costello
The World of the Pronghorn by Joe Van Wormer
The World of the Raccoon by Leonard Lee Rue III
The World of the Red Fox by Leonard Lee Rue III
The World of the Red-tailed Hawk by G. Ronald Austing
The World of the Ruffed Grouse by Leonard Lee Rue III
The World of the Snake by Hal H. Harrison
The World of the Swan by Joe Van Wormer
The World of the White-tailed Deer by Leonard Lee Rue III
The World of the Wild Turkey by James C. Lewis
The World of the Wolf
     by Russell J. Rutter and Douglas H. Pimlott
The World of the Woodchuck by W. J. Schoonmaker
The World of the Wood Duck
     by F. Eugene Hester and Jack Dermid

The World of the
PORCUPINE

Text and Photographs by

David F. Costello

J. B. LIPPINCOTT COMPANY

Philadelphia & New York

ISBN–0–397–00449–4
COPYRIGHT © 1966 BY DAVID F. COSTELLO
THIRD PRINTING
PRINTED IN THE UNITED STATES OF AMERICA
LIBRARY OF CONGRESS CATALOG CARD NO. 66–16658

To Cecilia

Contents

Meet the Porcupine

IT HAS BEEN SAID that nothing is more peculiar than a porcupine. He waddles when he walks. He minds his own business. He runs from nothing. And he never starves. He is pigeon-toed and bowlegged. He has feet like a bear, teeth like a beaver, claws like a badger, and inner fur like the wool on a sheep. He has been accused of being stupid. But he can learn to manipulate his way out of a cage with fewer trials than can a monkey. He can swim, croon a love song, climb the tallest tree, sleep like Somnus, and eat with his hands.

The porcupine has been the subject of innumerable legends, most of them false. It has been said that porcupines deliberately throw their quills, breed in the position of sloths, never suckle their young, destroy more forests than fires, insects, and disease put together, and frequently save the lives of people lost in the woods. It has been said that they are protected by law, that they are born without quills, that they go practically naked in winter, and that they have no natural enemies.

Most of these ideas are figments of the imagination or are based on stories that have increased in exaggeration with retelling through the years. Actually, the porcupine is one of the most fascinating animals that live in the woods.

The porcupine is a medium-sized mammal that belongs to the order Rodentia, which includes mice, squirrels, and beavers. Like other

11

Author and friend.

rodents, porcupines have a pair of upper and lower incisors which are used for gnawing wood and other materials that may serve as food. But they are best known for their sharp quills, which provide a remarkable defense against their enemies.

The name "porcupine" comes from the Latin *porcus*, "swine," and from the French *épine*, which came originally from the Latin *spina*, "thorn"; hence he is sometimes called a quill pig. The scientific name, *Erethizon dorsatum*, literally translated, means "the irritable back."

12

Meet the Porcupine

The porcupine is not a "hedgehog," a name properly applied to an entirely different European animal.

Porcupines characteristically are northern animals that inhabit forests from sea level to timber line. One porcupine was observed on Mount Rainier in western Washington at an elevation of approximately 14,000 feet. They are found at the northern limit of trees in the arctic, in the prairie of Nebraska, and occasionally in the desert in Arizona and Mexico.

Originally, porcupines were found in nearly all forested parts of the continent south to West Virginia, southern Illinois, the Davis Mountains of western Texas, and the southern end of the Sierra Nevada in California. They are not native to the southeastern states of the lower Mississippi Valley.

Wherever the porcupine may be, its quills indicate its degree of composure. When sleeping or eating or going about its business, it keeps its quills invisible and nicely flattened beneath its heavy coat of guard hairs. When disturbed, or threatened by enemies, it erects every quill. If attack is imminent, it thrashes its tail from side to side and even chatters its teeth.

The number of quills varies—some porcupines have more than 30,000; some have less. The quills, which usually are not more than 3 inches in length, are most numerous on the animal's tail and back. Occasionally they continue to the crown of the head, and sometimes they are found on the upper parts of the legs.

The undersurface of the body and insides of the legs are covered with fine short coat hairs mingled with longer coarse hairs. In winter the porcupine possesses woolly underfur mingled with the quills and obscured by the long guard hairs. The nose, cheeks and chin are densely covered with short coarse hairs. Vibrissae, or "whiskers," grow from the sides of the snout and cheeks. The undersurface of the tail is covered with short, very stiff bristles, which are securely attached to the skin.

13

The World of the Porcupine

The coloration of most porcupines is darker than one usually realizes. In photographing them, I have found it wise to increase the lens aperture one or two stops over what would be considered normal. Photoflash usually reveals even more details of the hairs and of the porcupine's head and face.

Hair color varies from black, with or without white-tipped guard hairs, to brown or chestnut. The guard hairs usually have bands of black and yellow of varying width. I have seen porcupines in Colorado that were greenish yellow and porcupines in British Columbia that were nearly black. A few pure albino porcupines have been reported.

The average adult porcupine is about 18 inches tall at the middle of its back when it is walking or standing on all four feet. When it sits on

Porcupine wandering in ponderosa pine country. The overgrazed range has few herbs, and the porcupine is forced to eat pine needles and bark, even in summer.

The porcupine always pulls away when held by the tail. The author stopped this one for examination in the sagebrush-juniper country in Central Oregon.

its haunches, propped by its tail, it is about 24 inches tall. Its body measures about 30 inches and its tail is from 6 to 10 inches long.

Porcupines show great variation in weight. Animals weighed in Massachusetts ranged from 5 to 13.5 pounds and averaged about 9 pounds. Thirteen porcupines weighed in Maine averaged 11.2 pounds. In Wisconsin, fifty-four adults averaged 14.3 pounds and twenty-eight adult females averaged 12.4 pounds. A female from King County, Washington, weighed 20 pounds.

I recently helped weigh a pet male porcupine at Prineville, Oregon, that tipped the scales at 28 pounds. Two female porcupines taken in Nebraska each weighed 27 pounds. I have been unable to ascertain the authentic weight of the heaviest porcupine on record since some published nonscientific reports are based on estimates rather than on weights obtained on reliable scales. Estimates usually are exaggerated, since live porcupines with quills and guard hairs erected appear to be

15

Pet porcupine nose-testing a carrot before eating.

Close-up shot of a porcupine face.

much larger than they really are. The average weight for healthy adults probably is about 15 pounds, but one author has cited the weight of an adult at 43 pounds.

Male porcupines are consistently heavier than females. In Arizona, Walter P. Taylor found that males averaged 22 per cent heavier than females. This tendency apparently holds for all the varieties of porcupines.

Porcupines grow throughout life, so an old porcupine, otherwise in good health, is generally the heaviest of all. Weight also varies with the season. In autumn, porcupines usually have stored a considerable

When a porcupine is looking for food, it keeps its nose close to the ground. This one is in Douglas fir region of western Washington.

Fences are a nuisance for porcupines. They could easily climb over, but persist in trying to go through, sometimes for an hour or more.

amount of fat. By midwinter most specimens are not fat. Porcupines living at low elevations where herbaceous food is abundant for a longer period average a few pounds heavier than those at higher elevations, especially those found above timber line in mountainous country.

Male and female porcupines resemble each other. Their sex cannot be told by casual examination. The nipples of the female can be seen during the nursing period. At other times, the animal must be examined closely before its sex can be determined.

Porcupines do not move rapidly, and they are experts in the art of relaxation. On the ground, they can sleep like cocker spaniels, with stomach to the ground and feet turned with soles upward. Aloft, they can sleep completely at ease with feet hanging down on either side of a branch or tree limb.

Some people have assumed that porcupines are stupid because they sleep most of the day. Being nocturnal animals, porcupines do most of their feeding and traveling at night when people do not see them.

Porcupines do not gnaw bark every time they climb a tree. In fact, many "roost" trees, where they sleep in the daytime, are never touched for food purposes.

Porcupines spend little time combing their hair. Occasionally they lick their paws. Sometimes they scratch, rather ineffectually, at loose quills that have lodged on their sides or belly. The animal is so stockily built and so structured that it is impossible for it to use teeth or claws in dressing the fur and hair on its back and tail.

19

The author uses this wire cone to catch and hold porcupines on the ground. They are easily released through the small end of the cone.

The porcupine is capable of shaking itself somewhat like a dog. This dislodges loose quills and hairs that are being shed, especially at molting time. Quills and guard hairs that are not being shed are under complete muscular control. The animal simply has to erect and then relax them to accomplish the job of hair straightening and grooming.

Porcupines have a remarkable sense of balance. In spite of their weight, they can strip leaves from branches no larger than your little finger without danger of falling from their lofty perches. Their long claws, bearlike feet, and sturdy tails enable them to climb saplings or giant trees with nearly equal ease.

They make interesting pets. They are playful creatures, especially when young. Even old porcupines can be tamed and taught to respond

20

to their names and to do tricks. Feeding them is no problem since they like all kinds of vegetables, herbaceous plants, fruits, nuts, and bread scraps from the table. If properly handled, they are gentle and enjoy being fed both by children and adults.

The porcupine's stomach can hold about a pound of food. The amount varies, of course, with the size of the porcupine and the time of year. A greater weight of herbaceous material is eaten in summer than of woody material in winter. A day's meal for a large porcupine in the forest is a patch of pine bark about the size of a sheet of typing paper. One of my pet porcupines could eat one-half pound of carrots and lettuce without stopping.

As an aid to digestion of bark and other woody material, the porcupine has about 25 feet of intestine. The intestine usually has a number of internal parasites in addition to the bacterial flora which undoubtedly assists in the digestion of cellulose in the same manner as with deer and other ruminants. The fermented wood odor of the porcupine originates in part from the digestive process.

Various authors disagree about the porcupine's intelligence and the acuteness of its senses. The common conclusion is that the animal is

This porcupine wants to climb back into the ponderosa pine. Note the reflection of sunlight on the long guard hairs.

dull, witless, and generally unaware of its surroundings. Laboratory studies of porcupine mentality, however, indicate that they adapt more readily to changed conditions than most animals.

They have excellent memories. Their senses of touch and smell are acute, and their hearing for certain sounds is equal to that of human beings. They are markedly curious about moving objects, although nonchalant in avoiding possible enemies.

Most people who have kept porcupines as pets agree that each animal has a distinct personality. Porcupines may be playful, morose, shy, or friendly and gentle. Occasionally they quarrel among themselves, but never actually fight.

Porcupines do not see well at distances of more than a few yards, but they readily see moving objects like men or dogs. At times it is almost impossible to photograph a wild porcupine head-on since it watches

Porcupine about five months old. When picked up by the tail, porcupines hold their hind paws together but try to grasp objects with their front paws. Author examining this one in central Oregon desert.

Porcupine in cultivated field.

every movement and always keeps its tail and back toward the camera-man. Approaching men and animals are almost always identified first by sound and by odor.

Walter P. Taylor states: "It is not improbable that the sense of smell is used: (1) to help find acceptable food; (2) to identify other animals, predecessors at porcupine trees and elsewhere, like the odor posts of the dog tribe; (3) to assist in mating activities; (4) to enable individual porcupines to keep their distance."

The female regularly gives birth to one young at a time, not two, or three, or four as has been reported in some magazine articles. Taylor states: "The frequency of twins must be of the order of once in perhaps three hundred to five hundred pregnancies. No authentic records of more than two young at a birth are at hand."

But Taylor did not publish any actual record of twins, showing date, location, or other circumstances. On the other hand, innumerable pregnant females have been examined by wild-life biologists and zoologists and the finding has always been the same—a single fetus. An examination of 54 porcupines from the Nicolet National Forest in Wisconsin, for example, showed that 20 were pregnant females, and each had a single embryo.

23

Meet the Porcupine

The nearest relatives of the porcupine inhabit the forests of tropical America from Mexico to Brazil. These porcupines, which have shorter quills than ours, are also smaller and more slender. Their outstanding characteristic is a prehensile tail, which is naked near the end. This allows the animals to cling to branches like an opossum. These tropical porcupines spend much more time in trees than our porcupines, which like to wander on the ground.

Still different porcupines are found in Europe, Asia, and Africa. Some of these have much longer quills and guard hairs. The African crested porcupine, *Hystrix galeata*, has 18-inch brown and white quills and black fur on the body. A crown of stiff bristles which can be erected along with the quills grows from the head to the shoulders. These porcupines can run like a dog and are belligerent when molested. Published reports state that when cornered they will attack by running backward. They are found together more than our American porcupines.

Our own more sedate porcupines are not gregarious animals, although several may be found together in permanent dens in winter. The attraction of a woodland camp with its odors of food and the availability of salt-impregnated articles often brings several porcupines together. This is one manifestation of their excellent sense of smell. But the only time when porcupines are commonly found in pairs is during the breeding season in autumn.

Any forest without native animals would echo with emptiness. When the camper comes home from a trip in the woods, his clearest memory frequently is that of the porcupines pottering around his camp at night. He especially remembers the porcupine that got into his tent or the one that roused him from sleep by clattering the pots and pans.

Many of my recollections of porcupines are vivid because of the circumstances under which the animals were encountered. The first por-

Porcupines in Oregon, Idaho, and Utah commonly migrate between sagebrush summer feeding grounds and pine-covered hills and buttes for winter feeding. Grizzly Butte in background, near Madras, Oregon.

Telephoto shot of porcupine in juniper. This animal watched the author 40 feet below. Note tail being used as a brace and nose testing the air for odors.

26

Porcupine camouflage. Even in a tree with few leaves, their lack of movement makes them inconspicuous.

27

The World of the Porcupine

cupine I ever saw was in the Bitterroot Mountains in Idaho, more than thirty years ago. The reverberation of its gnawing on a wooden leg of my camp cot at midnight startled me exceedingly. An hour of exasperation followed. It would not be chased away from the cot, which had become impregnated with salt after several years of storage in our eastern Nebraska smokehouse, where my father cured his meat each autumn.

Several years later I slept under the stars on that same cot in southern Wyoming. Apparently it still retained the savory odor of the smokehouse. I chased off five porcupines (I counted all of them at one time with the aid of my flashlight) in the early part of the night. In final desperation, I folded my bed and slept in the car until daylight.

Most of the porcupines I have seen have been in wooded country. Their preference for forested habitat is partly based on winter food needs. When trees are available and the snow is deep, no porcupine ever needs to starve.

Porcupines, however, are found far out on the plains and prairies. I knew one that wandered about the Central Plains Experimental Range in the short-grass vegetation north of Greeley, Colorado. During warm weather its food consisted of a great variety of herbaceous and low woody plants, including pentstemons, prickly-pear flowers, rabbit brush, and willow branches and leaves. When winter came, it lived on the bark of a cottonwood tree until spring.

Spring

ACROSS THE LAND the timetable for spring varies with geography. The green things of earth awaken early in the Arizona foothills, later in the Maine woods, and still later, but quickly, in the Far North with the breakup of ice on ponds, lakes, and rivers. The porcupines, without hibernating, have lived through the snows and icy blasts of winter with the wolves, lynxes, snowshoe rabbits, and deer. Now they come down from their cramped quarters in trees or forsake the dens which have sheltered them during winter storms and begin their travels.

They do not hurry. Their food supply of pine, or fir, or beech, or maple bark is nearby, and there is no reason to leave it until spring is assured. Birthing time is still weeks or months away. But the body fat, stored from the bountiful harvest of the previous autumn, is gone. Like most of us, the porcupine probably craves a change of diet as the kindly sun awakens the green things of earth.

Since her young one will be bound to the ground for a while after birth, the female porcupine stays near easily accessible food and a place of sanctuary for her young one from storms and enemies. Her spring wanderings are in search of more succulent herbs and tender browse than are generally available in dense forests. Openings in the forest, greening meadows, and pond edges with crisp water plants are places of choice.

29

The World of the Porcupine

In mountainous country where winter is king even in late spring, porcupines follow upward a few weeks behind the retreating snow line. Those that have braved the winter at high elevations occasionally migrate downward to greener pastures, or simply wait for the late coming of spring.

In spite of their slow locomotion, porcupines are great gypsies. Even if their travels are confined to a home territory, they move about a great deal. They spend their nights feeding and wandering. In the daytime, they rest in trees or in secluded places where they are not easily seen. This is especially true of porcupines of the eastern United States and Canada which seem not to migrate as extensively as western porcupines.

In the Pacific Northwest, the spring movement of porcupines in parts of the Cascade Mountains and the mountains in eastern Oregon is a slow deliberate movement from cliffs, lava rims, and pine forests downward to mountain meadows and valley farms. On the other hand, the porcupines in the Steens Mountains of southeastern Oregon spend their winters among the cottonwoods and willows along the streams and migrate back to the highlands as herbaceous plants begin growth in the spring. They prefer cottonwood bark and willow twigs to the juniper and sagebrush bark, which would be their only food at high elevations.

Good porcupine country contains a combination of conifers, shrubs, and open spaces with herbaceous plants for summer food and rocks for denning and shelter.

Agoseris flowers, a good substitute for dandelion heads in late summer in the mountains. Porcupines eat the heads but apparently do not like the leaves.

Porcupine food—pine needles. Many people do not realize that porcupines eat needles as well as bark.

These local shiftings of western porcupines are quite common. They have been observed in Colorado, Wyoming, Utah, Montana, Idaho, and British Columbia. Short migrations have been observed in the Goose Lake region of California and near Klamath Lake in southern Oregon.

According to C. Hart Merriam, the porcupines in the San Francisco Mountain region descend to lower levels in winter and return to the mountains in spring. Walter P. Taylor has reported numerous other instances of porcupine movements in Arizona and northern New Mexico.

Plains prickly-pear flowers are eaten by porcupines in eastern Colorado, miles from the nearest trees.

The World of the Porcupine

Ira N. Gabrielson found porcupines in the Crater Lake region in Oregon moving from rockslides to mountain meadows and irrigated ranches in late spring and summer. He suggested the possibility that the softening of quills by wet weather increases the animals' vulnerability to enemies and thus hastens their return to rocky ledges and dens in early fall.

Travel-ways used in migrations are difficult to identify unless one is thoroughly familiar with the local country. Evidences are lines of damaged trees and porcupine pellets beneath the trees. Taylor has suggested examination of the forest with field glasses from a high vantage

Porcupine scar on ponderosa pine is about five years old.

Recent porcupine scar, about one week old, on noble fir.

point to determine the location of spike-topped or malformed trees, followed by later intensive studies of specific areas.

Many studies have shown that travel-ways are most common in areas of varied topographic relief where mountain ridges and gulches provide convenient avenues for migration. On relatively flat land, porcupine travel-ways are ill defined or nonexistent, and the animals are widely distributed, especially with the approach of birthing time.

Spring

Much of our information about the development of infant porcupines immediately after birth has been obtained through observation of babies taken by Caesarean operation. Female porcupines that have just been killed are often examined by biologists for internal parasites and for evidence of pregnancy. Occasionally a fetus is found that has nearly reached full term. When carefully handled, this baby frequently

Porcupine scar on ponderosa pine in northern New Mexico. The animal sat on the different branches as it gnawed.

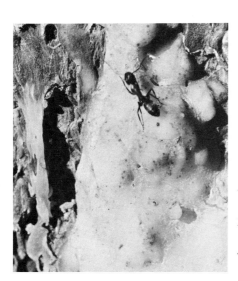

Resin from an old scar caused by porcupine's chewing on a ponderosa pine. Thatching ants apparently find food substances in these resin exudates.

begins to breathe and is able to walk within the hour. Taken at this stage, it makes an admirable pet and provides wonderful opportunities for study of the early childhood of the porcupine.

I have found no report of anyone observing the natural birth of a porcupine in the wild. Some years ago, Albert R. Shadle reported the birth of a baby porcupine to a captive female at the University of Buffalo. Dr. Shadle at that time believed it to be only the second case on record of a porcupine birth in captivity.

33

Nine-week-old pet porcupine eating potato chips. This one was obtained by Caesarean section.

At birth, this particular baby's eyes were open, its incisor teeth were well developed, its long hair was black, and its quills were present. It soon exhibited the usual porcupine defense reactions. But on continued association with people, it became tame and playful. It nursed until it was three and one-half months old.

One spring I periodically photographed a porcupine baby delivered by Caesarean operation by Maynard W. Cummings who then worked for the Fish and Wildlife Service of the U. S. Department of the Interior. Maynard and his wife, Juanita, named the baby Boris. Within half an hour after birth Boris walked. His quills were sharp as soon as he became dry.

34

Spring

For several days he was given milk with a medicine dropper. He soon graduated to a doll's nursing bottle with a nipple, and later to a larger bottle. When he was two-thirds as large as the family cocker spaniel, he still drank milk avidly.

The children gave him many kinds of food, but his favorite was potato chips. He loved dandelion and clover blossoms, and by midsummer he had learned to trim the rosebushes and to eat bark from the elm tree in the yard. When he started to remodel the chair legs and other furniture in the house and to chew on leather shoes, the Cummings family decided to return him to the woods. It was a sad time for all.

Numerous authors have described their interesting experiences with porcupine babies, which almost always make lovable pets. They are

Porcupine eating at the base of a beech tree in Pennsylvania.

The World of the Porcupine

easily started on cow's milk and soon learn to eat fruits, vegetables, and cereals. As they grow larger, they are able to hold oranges, apples, and corn on the cob in their front paws while they sit on their haunches.

They are playful and like to be handled if they are picked up with hands under their bodies rather than by their tails. They even like to be picked up by the forepaws and to be carried about in one's arms. At several months of age they still enjoy a romp on the lawn. And all during their babyhood and adolescence, they like to follow the people with whom they have been raised.

In the wild, the best evidence indicates that the young porcupine is born on the ground in a sheltered place such as a brush pile, under a protecting log, under the exposed roots of a fallen tree, or in a rock

Dandelion heads—favorite porcupine food.

Porcupine food—mountain mahogany.

den. It is questionable if a "nest" is ever deliberately made by the mother.

Most porcupine babies weigh about one pound at birth and have a total length of 11 or 12 inches. The tail is about 2½ inches, and the feet are usually less than 1½ inches in length. The baby is much blacker than its mother.

The majority of porcupines are born in April, May, and June. This variation in time of birth is to be expected since the breeding season covers a span of several months in the previous fall. If breeding occurs in mid-October, for example, the gestation period of approximately seven months will result in birth sometime in May in the following year.

Young porcupines have been found as early as February and as late as October. These are the exceptions. In the Southwest, most porcupines are born in April or May—the higher the altitude, the later the date.

The early childhood of the porcupine is concerned primarily with eating, seeking shelter, sleeping, and acquiring skills in climbing. Although young porcupines are precocious animals, reports that they almost immediately become independent of their mothers are probably exaggerations. This supposition of independence undoubtedly is based on the fact that the mother and young are so seldom encountered together in nature.

A study in Minnesota by Marshall *et al.* using radio-positioning techniques indicated that a mother porcupine and her daughter apparently had "some means of communication that enabled these 2 animals to locate each other, often from considerable distances." In the period, June 13 to July 16, "Fifty-two simultaneous daylight observations showed that the young porcupine remained within an average horizontal distance of 86 feet from her mother, with a maximum distance of 195 feet." Although the individual activity patterns of mother and young were erratic, the significant finding of this study is that the movements of the daughter paralleled those of the mother and that they were in communication with each other over a period of several weeks.

The use of miniature transmitters and portable radio signal-locator equipment on porcupines would provide much data on their movements, habitat preferences, choice of food, and use of ground and tree shelters. Eventually such studies may dispel much of the speculation about porcupine nursing habits and care of the young by their mothers.

Our best knowledge of nursing habits, of course, has been obtained from captive porcupines which have been observed to nurse until they are two or three months of age. In nature they undoubtedly supplement their milk diet at an early age with succulent herbs. A porcupine taken by Caesarean section on the Gunnison National Forest in Colorado ate blades of grass and dandelion blossoms at the age of two weeks.

Young porcupines are credited with eating tree seedlings which are only a few inches high. I do not doubt this, but the whole blame should not be put on porcupines. Mice, rabbits, and other animals also destroy many seedlings.

The young female porcupine that was repeatedly located by Marshall's group with radio signal-locator equipment furnished much information about the behavior pattern of these immature animals. Unlike the mother, the young animal moved about in the daytime, both on the ground and in trees.

She repeatedly used low dense vegetation as cover. "In most cases she was huddled against a log, stump, or at the base of a large tree. Once she was under a pile of slash."

During the period of study, she was observed in thirty-nine individual trees and shrubs consisting of nine different species. Jack pine, aspen, and red maple were the preferred resting trees. The authors state that "during June, the young porcupine was nearly always found on the trunk of a tree at heights of 6 to 8 feet above ground. Here the

A porcupine eating grass seeds. Note the guard hairs, some of which are eight to ten inches long.

38

animal was well concealed in the canopy of hazel underbrush, being hidden by several inches of dense foliage both above and below. During July, after its weight had increased to 2.0 kg., this porcupine started climbing to heights well above the hazel canopy."

Clarence Archer Tyron, Jr., reported the growth rate of a porcupine taken by Caesarean section in Montana in 1944. On May 20 it weighed 21 ounces. Some of the weights that followed were: June 1, 24 ounces; July 5, 41 ounces; August 8, 62 ounces; August 15, 110 ounces; and December 29, 185 ounces. On August 18, 1946, it weighed 250 ounces, or slightly more than 15.6 pounds. The growth rate was particularly rapid between birth and seven months of age.

A great variety of food is taken by both young and adult porcupines. This is a mark of their adaptability to different conditions throughout their range.

Porcupine interrupted while feeding. Tail in readiness for defense and a few quills erected. It keeps a watchful eye on the intruder.

Porcupine walking. When traveling the body is held well above the ground, and the tail does not drag. (The tail does drag, however, when the snow is soft and deep.)

In New England, the inner bark of sugar maple is a favorite food. Other hardwoods used for food are white ash, beech, basswood, American elm, willow, aspen, and various species of birch. In early spring porcupines are fond of poplar catkins.

The succulent plants in ponds are relished by porcupines. They readily wade in shallow water for lily pads, water cress, and sedges. James D. Curtis and Edward L. Kozicky report that one animal was observed feeding on an aquatic liverwort, *Riccia fluitans.* The porcupine kept its tail erect while wading belly deep in the shallow pool.

Western porcupines in early spring consume considerable amounts of inner bark of ponderosa pine, lodgepole pine, tamarack, spruce, fir, alder, and aspen. As the season progresses and porcupine travels increase, they turn to shrubs and a wide variety of herbaceous plants.

Walter P. Taylor, reporting on porcupines in the Southwest, lists the following shrubs in the diet: gooseberries, plums, chokecherry, buffalo berry, elder, black haw, raspberry canes, and buckbrush (*Ceanothus*). A host of herbaceous plants are also eaten, including geranium, lupine, cinquefoil, wyethia, and lousewort.

41

JACK GROOM

A porcupine chewed away almost half of plywood signboard above and to right of this smokey bear sign. Porcupines love the glue in plywood.

Chewing job by a large porcupine. It sat on the ground and chewed to a height of 30 inches. Note the parallel tooth marks.

Stepladder used for more than climbing by a porcupine. Blue Mountains of eastern Oregon.

Spring

Pine needles and inner bark are still eaten in spring, especially if late snowstorms force the animals to leave the ground. Yellow pine mistletoe consumption also increases slightly as compared with winter use.

Charles Foster Batchelder has given us some instructive notes on the feeding habits and daily travels of a wild mother porcupine and her young. She made her den in the stone foundation of an old barn about a hundred feet from his house in Peterborough, New Hampshire.

In October, 1929, the mother and cub frequented his lawn and browsed extensively on the branches of young elms and a group of arborvitaes. In 1930, the mother browsed in large elms and an apple tree. Batchelder surmised that her actions in the previous year were for the purpose of teaching the cub to climb.

The mother porcupine climbed a large limb of an elm tree by stretching all four legs around it. Then, "she reached up with her right arm, followed instantly with her left. Gripping with them, she swung her hind limbs simultaneously upward beneath her body, a surprisingly long swing, and from this new hold immediately repeated the action in the same order, traveling upward at a speed that seemed surprisingly rapid for an animal of her weight and apparent clumsiness."

The climbing of her small cub was observed on August 7, 1931. "He climbed slowly and hesitatingly, feeling his way, showing no trace of the firm, assured 'gait' of his mother. He reached out his hand and tried several tentative holds before he obtained a grasp to which he dared trust his weight. His air of inexperience and timidity as a climber contrasted strikingly with his mother's vigorous, rhythmic, almost automatic action, as she briskly pulled herself up the tree. His hesitation and slow movements soon left him behind his mother whose voice was to be heard occasionally from some point far out of my sight in the branches overhead."

My own observations confirm these reports of the climbing ability of mature porcupines. The animals are certainly much more at home in

43

Tame porcupine eating clover leaves. Note white-tipped guard hairs, and the heavy undercoat that resembles wool. The guard hairs of the tail are white. The quills are all concealed except for a few above the tail.

the trees than a man, even when he is equipped with climbing tools and ropes.

One of my experiences occurred in a 50-foot juniper tree in central Oregon. I clambered up the sticky trunk to photograph a porcupine that was resting on a branch about three inches in diameter. As I approached, it moved outward until it was clinging to twigs no larger than my little finger.

When I attempted to dislodge it by shaking the branch with my foot, it reached repeatedly with its right paw, trying to grasp an adjoining cluster of branches. Apparently it intended to circumnavigate me and return to the tree trunk on another limb.

A particularly sharp jolt loosened its hold and caused it to hang upside down from its twigs. For a moment it was still. Then it backed

44

like a sloth until the limb was large enough for it to climb to an upright position.

Without hesitation it then returned to the tree trunk, climbed past my left arm, and settled down for a nap in the very top of the tree.

Porcupines ascend trees headfirst, moving deliberately, but not too slowly. They show no hesitation about going clear to the top since their feeding grounds frequently are among the smaller branches. They descend backward, essentially reversing the movements used in ascending.

They frequently sit on their haunches on medium- to large-sized limbs. Their forepaws are used to draw in slender branchlets for food. Stems one or two feet long may be held with one or both paws while the tender bark and leaves are being eaten.

The porcupine's feet, claws, and tail are admirably suited for walking, sitting, or climbing. The feet are placed flat on the ground like those of a bear or raccoon. The soles are bare and are roughened with reticulations and tiny knobs that help the animal in climbing among rocks or on rough bark.

There are four toes on the front feet and five on the hind feet, all with strong claws. The claws are especially useful when the animal climbs trees with very large trunks. They are also used for holding food when the porcupine is sitting on its haunches.

When the animal sits, it uses its tail as a prop. The bristle-like hairs on the undersurface act like climbing spurs when the porcupine is moving up or down a tree trunk. When walking on limbs or small branches, the tail also is used for balance.

Probably no feature of the porcupine has been more discussed or examined than its quills. Unlike most mammals, the porcupine has three types of hair: the short brown or black underfur, the long guard hairs, and the quills.

I can agree to some extent with Seton's assertion that quills are the secret of the porcupine's life. He wrote, "To specialize and grow quills

45

it has relinquished speed, cunning, and keenness of senses; all the revenues of its body seem to have been converted to the growing of these awful spines." Certainly, with its peculiar physical and mental characteristics, the porcupine could not exist without its quills. But its keenness of touch and its sense of smell equal that of many animals. Its hearing, for certain sounds, also is excellent.

The quills, or spines, cover most of the upper surface of the animal from the eyes to near the end of the tail. Each and every quill is under muscular control. They lie flat and point to the rear when the animal is calm and undisturbed. They can be erected instantly when danger threatens. Their physical properties have been compared to those of the shaft of bird feathers. They are tough, elastic, and smooth except for the scaled part near the tip. The lower part of the quill is soft and white, but the upper needle-sharp point, for a distance of half an inch or more, is hard and black. This black tip is well armed with scales.

The number of quills on an adult porcupine has frequently been cited as approximating 30,000. Seton and Godwin estimated the quills on an eastern porcupine at 100 per square inch on the head and tail and 140 per square inch on the body.

Their measurement of $12\frac{1}{2}$ square inches of armored area on the head, 16 square inches on the tail, and 240 square inches on the body indicated a grand total of 36,450 quills.

An exact count would be almost impossible, since some of the quills are small and are almost indistinguishable from hairs. In fact, even the hairs of the undercoat possess scales.

The scales are arranged on the quills like shingles on a roof. Black-tipped quills are generally scaled only on the pigmented area. Totally white quills are generally scaled only near their tips, while totally black quills are usually scaled for two-thirds of their length. The scales which I have examined under the microscope were not barbed like fishhooks.

The stiffer spines are located on the porcupine's back and on the

Find the porcupine. It's near the top of the tree at the right side of the picture. The dark spot at the top of the tree in the center is a clump of mistletoe.

upper surface of the tail. The quills on the sides of the body are more slender and flexible.

Quills, like hairs, have a bulblike base which is retained in a follicle. When a quill has fully developed, root closure occurs. Quill removal then usually does not result in bleeding.

In a study of the pelage of the porcupine, Donald S. Po-Chedley and Albert R. Shadle measured the follicle tension of coat hairs, guard hairs, and quills at different times of the year. Coat hairs, being very small, required only 8 grams tension for withdrawal in June and August, and 63 grams in January. Obviously, the hairs are less strongly attached at molting, which is completed in summer.

Guard hairs were more difficult to withdraw than quills. A tension of 138 grams was necessary for withdrawal in August and 178 in Janu-

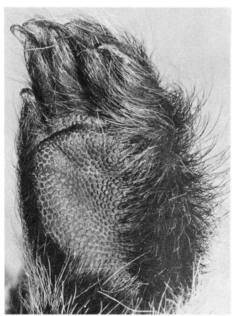 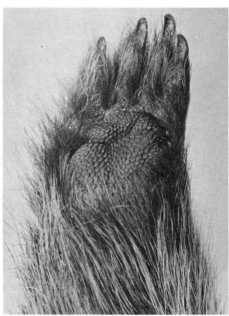

Hind foot of a porcupine showing the five claws. The feet are placed on the ground like those of a bear.

The front feet have four claws which are used for climbing and for holding various objects.

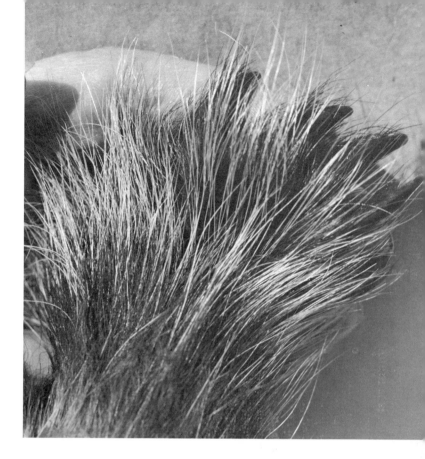

*The long guard hairs extend
beyond the claws.*

ary. Quills required 106 grams of tension for withdrawal in June and increasing amounts until January, when 146 grams was required.

As these authors point out, "The ease of withdrawal from the porcupine, the anchoring function of the scales of the quill, and the toughness of the skin of the other animal cause the ready transfer of the quills of the porcupine to its victim."

Once, in handling a porcupine that had been killed by an automobile, a single quill punctured the thumb of my right hand to a depth of about ¼ inch. My thumb had been hardened by work in the woods, and I was unable to remove the quill with the fingers of my left hand. There was no pain until a companion helped remove the quill. The puncture bled for a few minutes, and a slight soreness persisted for about two hours. No disinfectant was used, and no infection developed.

Do porcupines replace quills that are lost? The answer is yes.

When quills are lost or removed they are gradually replaced. New quills start to develop within a few days and grow at the rate of about

49

Porcupine in defense posture—ready to strike upward with tail.

½ millimeter per day. The new growth may continue for two to eight months.

In spite of the porcupine's quills and its deliberate actions, it is not the animal moron so often described in the hunting magazines and forestry literature. In fact, it is a rather sensitive creature which responds to patience, kindness, and firmness when handled by people. Dr.

Pet porcupine allows its teeth to be shown.

When a porcupine walks it waddles since its legs are set far apart and it is bow-legged. Red alder woods in western Washington.

Albert R. Shadle, who studied them for many years, wrote: "Never mistreat porcupines! They remember such experiences sometimes for weeks or months, and it may require considerable time and training to undo the results of one such bad experience."

Mrs. Jim Elkins, who has raised several porcupines at Prineville, Oregon, tells me that each one has a distinct personality and has to be handled differently. My own observations of two of her porcupines, and of porcupines in the wild, tend to confirm this. Her old male porcupine, which weighed 28 pounds the last time I saw him, was gentle and affectionate and could be lifted and carried around by his front feet. Mrs. Elkins could even grab him by the snout and spread his lips to show me his teeth. On the other hand, her young female porcupine was moody, irascible, and disdainful of any human contact.

A wild male porcupine that I recently kept as a pet learned to eat carrots and bread from my hand within two days after his capture. He showed a definite preference for my wife and would go to her for pro-

52

Porcupine resting in red alder tree. The catkins of alders and willows are eaten by porcupines.

tection when I interfered with his activities while taking photographs.

One characteristic common to porcupines is persistence. When they set out to do a certain thing, it appears that nothing short of death will deter them from attainment of their objective.

One porcupine that I watched periodically from spring until late summer in 1964 persistently rested in a juniper tree near Madras, Oregon. When I would surprise it on the ground, it would erect its quills and go through defense motions if approached too closely. All the while, it would be moving among trees of various sizes. Even though I diverted it over rock piles, through sagebrush, or across a small creek, it ultimately succeeded in climbing its favorite tree.

53

The World of the Porcupine

Donald A. Spencer demonstrated the persistence of porcupines with an electric fence built to control their movements on the Mesa Verde National Park, Colorado. The first contact of the porcupine's nose with the charged wire always made it whirl with tail toward the fence and all quills raised. After two or three attempts to climb the fence, the porcupine would then test the wire with a paw instead of its nose. Spencer watched a porcupine make five attempts to climb an electric fence in two hours.

James D. Curtis states: "Porkies have been seen testing glare ice on a sidehill five times with a front foot before venturing onto it. And on more than one occasion when released some distance from their point of capture, they have been observed to run—yes, run—in a beeline for their dens. No, they are not completely stupid."

A porcupine that frequented a girls' camp in California learned to open doors with its claws. I have seen several captive porcupines that would extend a paw to shake hands with people.

The playfulness of young porcupines has been described many times. They play with movable objects. They tussle with one another. They bite harmlessly at fingers, and they love to have their bellies tickled.

Baby porcupines will hump their backs like a cat, walk stiff-legged, and then spin as if they were on a pivot. The tones of their squeaky voices have been known to rise and fall with the emotions and enthusiasm engendered by play. Porcupines nearly a year old still retain some of the desire to play.

In a study of animal behavior, L. W. Sackett found porcupines adaptable to widely different circumstances whether young or old. They were much more adaptable to change in place and time of experiments than raccoons. Porcupines also solved the maze problem more readily than other animals used in his experiments.

Other research workers have found the porcupine's mentality slow but tenacious. Once they have learned a procedure or have developed

*Head and shoulders of an old porcupine with heavy underfur. Its ear is about
2 inches above the eye in the illustration. It is using its nose to locate clover leaves
among the grass blades.*

55

Porcupine reaching for lilac flowers. Note the incisor teeth and the four claws on the front foot.

a response to a certain stimulus, they are not likely to forget it.

In the wild, porcupines are particularly adaptable to changes in their environment. If timber cutting, cultivation, road building, or other cultural practices change their habitat, they readily establish new routes of travel, find new resting places, and explore the territory for new kinds of food.

Their explorations bring them to new crops in season such as lush alfalfa stands, cornfields when the corn is in roasting ear stage, and wheat prior to ripening and harvest. Man-made structures are tested for palatability, whether they be sugar barrels in Vermont or saddle blankets in California.

If a salt-impregnated article is available in a porcupine's territory, the porcupine is apt to find it. The man-made articles sampled by porcupines are innumerable, and include leather, rope, tables, toilet seats, wooden furniture, shoes, automobile tires, plywood signs, aluminum pans, fences, and cabins. This fondness for salt appears to be greatest in spring.

No one has satisfactorily explained the porcupine's ability to locate salt-impregnated articles. I suspect that their sense of smell leads them more than has been recognized. They probably are attracted by odors of other substances that are mixed with salt. Usually only the porcupines in a limited territory come to any particular place where salt is found.

The seasonal territories of porcupines vary greatly in different parts of the country. The winter range of the animal in New England has been reported at about six acres with a mean radius of about 300 feet. In spring and summer the animals wander farther in search of food. Males have been recovered 5 miles away from den sites where they were tagged.

In the Lake States, thirteen tagged porcupines were recaptured over a year's time. The average distance between point of tagging and recapture was 2,716 feet or about one-half mile. Six males averaged 3,300 feet while the females averaged only 2,216 feet.

Similar observations made in winter in New York showed porcupine movements ranging from 26 to 3,190 feet, averaging 430 feet. From these data the winter feeding area was estimated at approximately 13 acres.

In early summer, two porcupines in Minnesota, followed by radio-positioning techniques, traveled maximum distances of 840 and 850 feet in one night. Minimum distances recorded were 30 and 90 feet respectively. Over a 30-day period these two animals remained in areas of 32 and 36 acres.

Stag-top ponderosa pine caused by porcupine girdling.

In Oregon, Ira N. Gabrielson found porcupines visiting mountain meadows in spring and summer after having spent the winter in rockslides. He believed that the spring movement covered several weeks of aimless wandering over a rather limited territory.

Hudson G. Reynolds observed a porcupine sleeping in a mescat acacia, *Acacia constricta,* in the desert-shrub habitat in Arizona. The nearest ponderosa pine forests were in either the Pinal or the Catalina Mountains, more than 40 miles away. He concluded that further observation and evidence was needed before it could be decided that this porcupine's habitat was year-long, seasonal, or casual.

From many studies and observations it is apparent that porcupines, particularly the western varieties, make migrations especially in spring and fall. It also appears that when they come to the end of their migration they change to a stay-at-home status and do much wandering in a limited territory.

58

Summer

SUMMER IS THE TRAINING TIME for young porcupines. A few are born in March and April. Many of them arrive in May and June, in time to take advantage of the natural profusion of edible plants which soon become their entire diet as weaning is accomplished.

Since permanent dens are seldom used in summer, the young porcupines, cubs, or porcupettes, as they are sometimes called, spend their days and nights learning about shelter, resting places, and good things to eat.

Their world is filled with the strange magic of new sights, sounds, and odors. There are new sensations to experience—the taste of mother's milk, the beat of rain, the damp of night, the sting of mosquitoes, and the sounds of other animals.

In the northern woods the sweets of wild sarsaparilla and pennyroyal, the biting taste of jack-in-the-pulpit, the stinging cysts of nettles, and the somber flesh of cohosh and Seneca snakeroot are there for trial. In the forest openings the pungent juice of yarrow, the stringy fibers of hemp, and the towering stems of Joe-Pye weed are secrets to be tested with teeth and tongue. Along with these are hundreds of other plants and objects to be sampled in the grand exploration.

This prodigality of nature is the same everywhere. In the Rocky Mountains, where I made botanical surveys for several years, each major vegetation type included no less than 600 characteristic plant species. It was not unusual to find 50 to 75 conspicuously different plants on an acre of ground.

This abundance of natural food makes it unnecessary for the porcupine mother and cub to travel far in their daily rounds. The ease of getting a full belly allows the cub time for solitary exploration, time for sleeping, and time for learning to climb trees. Through all this training period, the mother stays within communicating distance of her young one, but she travels more widely in search of food.

One summer in the Bighorn Mountains in Wyoming, I watched a porcupine mother, who left her cub in hiding, regularly come out of the spruce forest each morning to graze in a lush mountain meadow. She was a big handsome animal with golden-greenish pelage. The profusion of forage gave her so many choices that I never determined all the plants she used.

She regularly ate agoseris flower heads, which are similar to dandelion flower heads. American bistort, alpine bluebells, alpine buttercup, mountain clover, and dwarf willows were definitely on her menu.

Western porcupine country—big, wild, and beautiful.

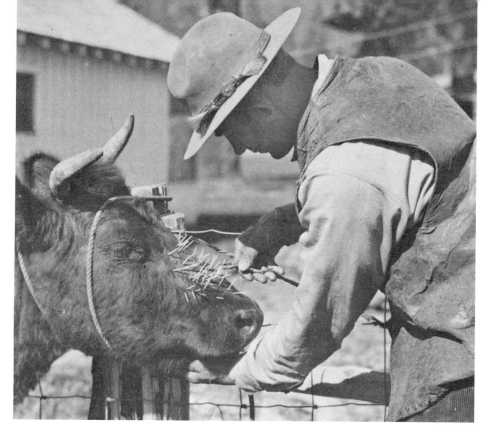

Cow with quills. Domestic livestock are quilled occasionally as a result of smelling at porcupines out of curiosity.

I could not see if she ate any of the numerous bluegrasses, sedges, and rushes which grew in the moist places. But she had a wide selection since a botanical survey of the meadow indicated the presence of more than 100 grasses, weeds, and shrubs available for grazing.

The abundance of food in mountain meadows and grasslands is the principal factor that causes nocturnal movements of porcupines from the woods in summer. If undisturbed, a porcupine will make nightly forays to lush grazing areas and return by the same route to a favorite daytime resting tree.

Apparently porcupines become familiar with game trails, stream sides, and easily followed runways that lead to good feeding grounds. When out in the open they remain oriented to the forest and to places for hiding or sleeping when necessity demands.

Several years ago in the South Park country of Colorado, I watched a mature porcupine as it meandered slowly, and apparently erratically, through a stand of Arizona fescue and other bunchgrasses. I surmised that it was searching for the occasional specimens of Fremont geranium and American vetch which were about the only other palatable plants in evidence.

The animal sensed my presence at a distance of more than 100 feet, probably from the crunching of gravel beneath my boots. It immediately started in a fast waddle, not toward the spruce trees 50 yards ahead, but diagonally toward a low rock rim nearly 150 yards to the left. When it arrived there, it unerringly found its way to a deep crevice in the outcrop and quickly disappeared from my sight into the rocks.

The wandering ability of the porcupine is sure to bring it to some strange foods. It seems willing to test anything edible and some things not edible. Numerous accounts have been given of porcupines gnawing aluminum pans and plastic dishes in summer camps. They are attracted by deer antlers, salt, grease, and soap. There is one report of a porcupine that ate a quantity of chloride of lime and apparently survived with no harmful results.

Fruit trees are occasionally damaged by porcupines. In central Oregon they ate watermelons. Gabrielson reported them feeding on carrots, lettuce, cabbage, and other truck crops.

Throughout the West, in addition to such staple foods as the bark of pines, Douglas fir, and willows, porcupines eat many green succulent foods which are rich in vitamin A in summer and early fall, prior to the onset of the breeding season.

Bark is readily taken from wild roses, wild cherry, serviceberry, and curl-leaf mountain mahogany. Herbaceous plants commonly chosen are wild clover, geraniums, mountain bluebells, goldenrods, asters, and dandelions.

Hudson G. Reynolds, in reporting an observation of a porcupine in the desert-shrub habitat of Arizona, states: "On the same day the sleeping porcupine was observed, an ocotillo with twelve 24-inch pieces of stem peeled from the main plant was seen nearby. Teeth

Telephoto shot of porcupine in top of tall juniper tree in central Oregon. Note the long claws on the forepaws.

63

Porcupine climbing. The animal comes down backward.

Porcupine climbing. One front foot is advanced while the others hold fast to the bark.

marks on the branches were too large to have been made by any rodent except a porcupine."

Benson, reporting on porcupines near Puerto Kino in Mexico, speculated that porcupines may eat paloverde, paloferre, and mesquite when they occupy desert-shrub habitats.

Taylor reports numerous instances of porcupines ranging various distances from forests in summer. One was observed in August in the overgrazed snakeweed plains south of Seligman, Arizona. Charles T. Vorhies found one in the desert-scrub country southeast of Tucson. M. E. Musgrave saw a porcupine on the open desert south of Bonita, Arizona. It was 10 miles from the nearest pine trees.

Vernon Bailey found porcupines in the sagebrush country in Wyoming 10 miles or more from timber. On the other hand, porcupines have been taken in the heart of Salt Lake City, Utah. They occasionally wander into the business district of Colorado Springs, Colorado, in summer.

This wanderlust tends to insure the porcupine the widest ecological range, so all favorable environments become populated. Obviously, during their summer travels, the food problem is minor, wherever they may be.

In all their wandering, adult porcupines seldom associate with one another. Not until the end of summer and the beginning of the restless season, prior to mating, are males and females found in the same places.

The mother and young remain fairly close together for many weeks after birth, although they are seldom seen at the same time. If the porcupine baby is found under a log, among ferns, under a brush pile, or in low shrubbery, the mother can sometimes be found by diligent examination of all the trees in the neighborhood.

The youngster travels more than its mother in the daytime. In the process of growing up, it eats more frequently of herbs, tree seedlings, and low shrubs. They both travel about their local neighborhood at night. If they are near human habitation, they may make nightly forays

65

The World of the Porcupine

from woods to cultivated crops. It also has been reported that mother porcupines and their young may make nightly runs to ponds and streams and back to their daytime resting places.

Weather, especially in summer, does not greatly influence porcupine habits or travels. Certainly, their abundance in a given locality seems to be governed more by reproductive rate, length of life, and natural enemies than by weather.

Porcupines have been observed repeatedly in rain. Damp weather in summer does not seem to drive them out of trees and into dry hollow logs or rocky dens. In fact, porcupines do not avoid water since they commonly wade in shallow ponds in search of succulent plants.

Even the extremes of winter appear to cause little discomfort. Many porcupines have been observed in the branches of trees during severe cold spells. Some have been known to remain in a single tree for several weeks through all the vicissitudes of blizzards and days of heavy snowfall.

Porcupine tracks in snow indicate that they travel during moderate periods between storms. Their trails during long stretches of subzero weather commonly lead to hollow logs or rocky dens, indicating they travel to and fro between food trees and shelter. Porcupines have been known to burrow through snow in order to reach windfalls or dens. Jacob Shapiro believes that shelter is sought more as a protection from wind and snow, and possibly from predators, than as a protection against cold.

Wild animals in general instinctively leave porcupines alone. But, of the thousands of foxes, raccoons, minks, and other fur bearers regularly taken by trappers in country heavily populated by porcupines, frequently one is found with quills. Coyotes, bears, and mountain lions which occasionally kill porcupines are sometimes quilled.

Porcupine in aspen in Dixie National Forest, Utah.

U. S. FOREST SERVICE

66

The World of the Porcupine

The porcupine's greatest natural enemy is the fisher. These animals belong to the weasel family and are about the size of large house cats. They prefer porcupine to almost any other meat and are extremely adept at killing their prey.

Originally the fisher's range encompassed the northern forests of the United States and Canada from coast to coast, with southward extensions in the coniferous timber of the higher mountains. They now exist mainly in the Canadian woods and the northern parts of Maine, New Hampshire, and New York. Recently, a few were liberated in Oregon, but no reports of the success of their establishment are available.

Fishers have been trapped extensively for their fine pelts. New York has managed the fisher as a valuable fur bearer and as a means of controlling porcupine numbers. At the time of World War I, a fisher pelt was worth 150 dollars. As the price declined to 5 or 10 dollars, the numbers of fishers increased. Twenty years ago they controlled an eruptive porcupine population in the Adirondack Mountains to the point where hardly a porcupine could be found.

The porcupine is a lot of meat for a small effort from the fisher. This agile animal is as much at home in the treetops as a squirrel, and it matters not to the fisher if the porcupine is aloft or on the ground. According to popular accounts, the fisher rips open the porcupine's soft underbelly with little danger from the quills. If the porcupine is on snow, the fisher is reputed to burrow up from below in order to attack the vulnerable areas of his prey.

Numerous reports tell of trappers finding porcupine pelts, quill sides down, laid out on the ground like bath mats by fishers. Most of the meat and bones are consumed. Scavenger animals and birds get the rest.

Among the porcupine's other natural predators are bobcats, bears, wolves, foxes, and occasionally the great horned owl and the eagle. There is one published report of a cougar that died as a result of seventeen imbedded porcupine quills. Some quills had penetrated its eyes

When a porcupine waddles, all its spines and hairs shake.

and the brain. Taylor reports that eagles have been found dead with quills lodged in vital spots.

Bears probably seldom attack porcupines for food. They may, however, touch a porcupine out of curiosity and get stuck with a few quills. This naturally results in a full-sized swat by the bear's paw and real trouble for the bear.

Cougars, or mountain lions, are often found with imbedded quills. Porcupine flesh has been found in samples of their stomach contents, and photographs have been published showing their scats almost completely filled with quills. It has been suggested that the digestive juices of the lion soften the quills so that the meal is not fatal. The manner in which a lion kills a porcupine is pure speculation.

69

The World of the Porcupine

Reports of trappers in Montana and in Canada tell that wolves caught in earlier days had porcupine quills in the neck and shoulders. One account states that wolves grab porcupines by the nose and shake them until they are dead.

K. D. Flock described weasel attacks on porcupines. One encounter was observed by him. In other instances, evidence in the snow indicated that the bloodthirsty little animal had slashed the porcupine's throat from beneath, where quills were few.

Coyotes can cleverly outwit porcupines. Generally they work in pairs and maneuver the porcupine to get it on its back so the vulnerable parts are exposed.

Bobcats and foxes caught in traps frequently have porcupine quills in various parts of their bodies. Evidences of struggle in the snow indicate that these animals are enemies of the porcupine. The presence of porcupine hair and quills in their stomachs, however, may only indicate that bobcats and foxes have been feeding on the carcasses of porcupines.

A. E. MacGregor, in an analysis of fox foods in Massachusetts, found that 9 per cent of the fox stomachs examined had porcupine quills that had penetrated the stomach wall. "Two fox skulls contained quills imbedded in the flesh against the skull."

Dogs are notorious for attacking porcupines. I doubt if many dogs ever succeed in killing porcupines, but some will tackle them again and again. The painful experience of being dequilled does not teach them to leave porcupines alone.

Man, of course, is the porcupine's worst enemy. Foresters in particular have a consuming hatred for them. Local control certainly is justified in many instances. But I have never been able to comprehend why some men will continue to beat the body of a porcupine long after it is dead, even when the animal is discovered in the sagebrush miles from a timber stand.

Mosquitoes, as vectors of nematodes, might be considered an enemy of the porcupine. There is considerable evidence that the animals in summer seek the heights of tall trees to escape these insect pests. Porcupines after their nocturnal foraging in bogs and swamps return to trees on the uplands for daytime protection from mosquitoes.

Paul R. Highby found that one species of nematode, *Dipetalonema arbuta*, parasitizes the porcupine in its peritoneal cavity and another, *Dirofilaria spinosa*, in its dorsal subcutaneous connective tissue. These parasites develop in the mosquito and can be transmitted to the porcupine.

Porcupines suffer from a variety of other parasites and diseases. Little is known, however, about the degree of mortality from pathogenic organisms.

The commonest external parasites are ticks and biting lice, but not all porcupines are infested by these pests.

There is one report in the literature, by Payne and O'Meara, of a porcupine affected with mange. When the animal was examined at the

Examining pellets from a log used for temporary shelter by porcupines. The log is not hollow, only the end has been burned out. It is used by porcupines during stormy periods when wind and snow blow. Blue Mountains in eastern Oregon.

The World of the Porcupine

University of Maine; it had encrustations on the legs and over most of the ventral surface of the body. Microscopic examination of the encrusted material revealed numerous mites, *Sarcoptes scabei*.

Porcupines, like men, grasshoppers, hogs, and rabbits, have roundworms and tapeworms. One porcupine had several hundred roundworms in its intestine, but appeared to be in reasonably good health.

Colorado tick fever has been isolated from a porcupine captured near Snowmass, Pitkin County, Colorado. Willy Burgdorfer injected an experimental porcupine with virus prepared by grinding infected wood ticks and found that the animal was susceptible to the fever. The infection did not cause obvious illness in the animal. It is probable that porcupines could infect other ticks that feed on them just as ground squirrels, pine squirrels, wood rats, chipmunks, and other rodents can transmit the virus.

Diseases and parasites are not the worst enemies of the porcupine. Sometimes I think the animal itself is its own worst enemy. It never attacks animals or men. But its armor of quills invites retaliation when curiosity or attack by other creatures provokes them to destructive action.

At times, even its voice leads to its undoing. Like a mumbling old man it sometimes announces its presence around camps at night and in the woods during the mating season. The porcupine does have a voice, and it has many variations and meanings. I have heard them murmuring beyond the shadows of my campfire from Yellowstone National Park south to Arizona and west to Oregon. Some of their sounds have been almost inaudible grunts. Others have been a pitiful whining, which by no means meant that the animal was in distress.

I have never heard a porcupine give the *coo-coo-coo* sound or the weak high yipping bark that others have described. But I have cuddled their babies in my hands and heard them murmur and grunt like an overfed puppy dog.

Once when I attempted to weigh a large porcupine, it lost its patience, hissed, chattered its teeth, and urinated copiously on the

72

Episode near Thompson Reservoir in southern Oregon in late evening. Dog discovers porcupine in mountain meadow; comes in for attack; porcupine presents back to dog, holds tail in readiness to strike dog.

platform of the scales. Obviously it was angered and disturbed by my attempt to guide it with a wooden leaf rake.

William Curtis states that on a fishing trip on the Scott River in California he heard a ghostly cry rise and dwindle away. With a flashlight he found the source of the wail, a young porcupine.

Albert R. Shadle, who made many scientific studies of many porcupines, stated: "When the males are sexually excited, they are likely to vocalize more or less. The 'singing' as we call it, may vary from an almost inaudible low whine in slight excitement, to a high pitched, piercing whine in an animal which is greatly excited.... Some males usually 'sing' in a low tone, some have a moderate whine, while others are so loud as to be almost disagreeable."

73

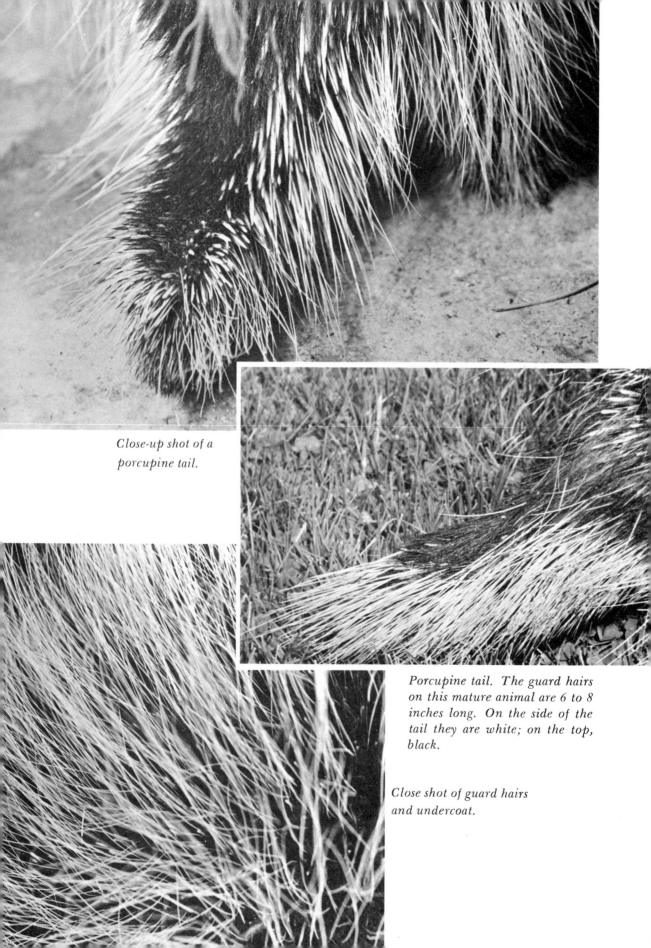

Close-up shot of a porcupine tail.

Porcupine tail. The guard hairs on this mature animal are 6 to 8 inches long. On the side of the tail they are white; on the top, black.

Close shot of guard hairs and undercoat.

Like many animals, porcupines occasionally can be called by imitating their voices. I have never succeeded in doing this, apparently because my "Unh, unh, unh" does not sound natural. Donald Spencer states that he once called a large porcupine out of a hard maple near Rhinelander, Wisconsin. "He waddled across 40 feet of snow-covered brush and fallen logs to stand at my feet." Part of the secret is in standing still, since porcupines pay little attention to motionless objects.

Voice communication is used by porcupine mothers and their young. With the coming of night, the mother descends from her daytime tree shelter. Although her infant may not approach her directly in response to her utterance, it sometimes answers with plaintive whimperings.

Porcupine mothers also use voice sounds to persuade their infants to leave their hiding places or to climb trees when the mother already is in the branches high overhead. I have found no record that the mother calls her young to suckle it or that she goes to her infant in response to its whimperings.

There is much speculation about the time and manner of weaning the young. Numerous publications state that the young porcupine is driven away soon after birth or that it is allowed to suckle for only a week. Walter P. Taylor cites an Indian legend that the mother porcupine never suckles her young.

Taylor states: "The weaning process must begin soon after birth. Indeed, each porcupine seems to be able to shift more or less for itself, even when quite young. The apparently minor role played by milk in the young porcupine's diet looks like an adaptation to early independence of the individual."

This opinion is supported by many observations of caged porcupines obtained by Caesarean operation. Although these captive animals avidly drink milk for several weeks, they are not exclusively dependent on it. Many baby porcupines eat green herbage within two weeks after

75

they are born. On the other hand, captive mother porcupines have been observed to suckle their young for three months or more after birth.

In the wild, female porcupines normally suckle their young for six or seven weeks. A few female porcupines have been found with milk as late as September or October. Their young, however, may have been born in late summer. Hence there is no reason to assume in these cases that suckling had continued to late fall from the usual birth time in April or May.

The association of mother and young is probably broken within a few weeks through normal wandering, through interference by enemies, and by storms. The little porcupine travels more on the ground than its parent, and sooner or later it is bound to lead an independent existence.

Both young and adult porcupines are sufficiently equipped by instinct and senses for effective existence in the wild. From their earliest moments in life the quick tail jerk and quill erection are automatically evoked by even a light touch on the guard hairs. The defensive reaction can even be produced by a quick puff of air.

The vibrissae, or whiskers, are especially sensitive to touch. They serve as guides when the animal is wandering at night or in caves or underground places. My observations of porcupines in trees indicate that the vibrissae also assist the porcupine in finding a passage through dense clusters of branches and twigs.

The tail also is used as a feeler to guide the porcupine in its descent from trees, since the animal nearly always goes down backward. Sometimes the tail is pressed against the bark in several places before the stiff bristles are pushed into place to help support the animal. I have seen porcupines do this on aspens, alders, and junipers which have relatively smooth bark.

The quills also are sensory receptors. One may demonstrate this by touching a single quill with a stick when the porcupine is quiet. The

This porcupine has started its wandering just before sundown in the Medicine Bow National Forest of southern Wyoming.

animal may lurch toward the stick or flail with its tail, depending on the location of the disturbed quill.

It is generally believed that porcupines have poor eyesight. Light from an electric torch does not easily disturb them. They pay little attention to the lights of an automobile. I have photographed them at close range with the aid of flash bulbs and have observed no particular reaction to the blinding light, although they have occasionally stopped eating for a few minutes.

I am convinced that porcupines can see reasonably well at close range. On various occasions when they were trying to escape from me

Porcupine climbing for willow catkins at 17 mile on the Steese Highway northeast of Fairbanks, Alaska.

SIGURD T. OLSON

in trees, they have reached with their paws for branches projecting from other tree limbs. I also have watched them go directly from one dandelion blossom to another in meadows without attention to wind direction which otherwise might have guided them by smell.

At distances of 50 feet or more, it is difficult to learn if the porcupine is made aware of moving objects by sight or by sound. Their sense of hearing for certain sounds is good, if not excellent. On many occasions I have seen them break into a fast waddle 25 to 50 yards away when they heard the crunch of gravel beneath my boots.

Charles Foster Batchelder, who recorded some fascinating notes on a female porcupine in New Hampshire from 1929 to 1933, states that she stopped and listened when an electric bell rang in the house some 80 feet away. On another occasion she stopped and then galloped into some shrubbery when someone coughed slightly in the kitchen.

Porcupines use their noses freely at all times. They regularly sit on their haunches to sniff the air. Food is practically always examined with the nose before a selection is made.

Many of the paths used in nightly travels are sprinkled with urine as are trees used for resting places. Whether the porcupine uses the sense of smell for guidance in these odoriferous situations is not known for certain.

Unusual odors seem to be readily perceived by porcupines. The scents used by trappers often attract porcupines to traps which have been set for coyotes and other animals. The ability of the porcupine to locate food in hunters' camps is legendary.

The porcupine itself has a strong body smell which somewhat resembles the odor of decayed wood. This odor is probably an aid for mutual attraction of males and females during the breeding season. On the other hand, Taylor suggests that the sense of smell, with the associated body odor, may enable porcupines to keep apart during the seasons of their solitary existence.

Summer is the time of molt for porcupines. The undercoat hairs are shed more or less *en masse*, beginning in late spring and ending in summer. This accounts for the bare skin that can be seen among the quills on the backs of porcupines found in August and September. Reports that the porcupine is practically bare in winter are largely untrue since the winter pelage is usually developed by late fall.

The quills are not shed *en masse*. If they were, the porcupine would be without protection for several weeks in midsummer. Instead, quill removal caused by contact with enemies or various objects is followed by the development of replacement quills, regardless of season.

Close examination of a porcupine will reveal quills in various stages of development. Some will be found to be emerging, others will be mature, some will be so loosely attached that they fall away when the animal shakes itself like a dog or violently switches its tail.

Reports of the effects of quills on animals and man are legion. Anyone who handles and studies porcupines sooner or later will have quills embedded somewhere in his anatomy. I have received quills in my hands even from gingerly handling dead porcupines. In the excitement of capturing a porcupine in a tree or pulling one by the tail from its den, one is liable to receive quills which work into the flesh without being noticed.

A published report by Albert R. Shadle describes the passage of a 7 mm. quill fragment through the skin and muscle of his arm. It traveled 42 mm. in 42 to 45 hours, or at the rate of about 1 inch per day. No infection developed, and only an occasional slight pricking sensation was felt while the quill was moving through his arm.

Shadle and Po-Chedley also reported on a mishap with a porcupine in the laboratory at the University of Buffalo. The animal fell from a table, and seventy-nine quills penetrated Po-Chedley's leg. All but one were immediately removed. The remaining quill disappeared beneath the skin. In 30.5 hours, "The contraction of the muscle, in contact with the scales on the embedded spine, drew the spine a distance of 32 mm. (1.05 mm. per hour) through the tissue to the point of emergence.... There was only slight discomfort resulting from the actual

80

A Colorado porcupine in midsummer. This one is in the Pike National Forest at an elevation of 8,000 feet.

81

passage of the quill through the tissue."

The relatively few quills I have acquired have never been embedded beneath the skin. But those which have been difficult to remove have left a slight soreness for a few hours. Some of my friends, however, who have had quills deeply embedded, experienced pain throughout the affected leg or arm.

A lot of hogwash has been written about how to remove a porcupine quill. Vinegar has been recommended for softening the spines. Clipping the quills to let the air in has been suggested. But most quills are not hollow-shafted.

Old woodsmen are credited with the suggestion that the quill be twisted, or "unscrewed." Microscopic examination of the scales reveals no spiral arrangement. Frederick V. Coville states, however, that the scales are not rigid and possibly would be bent to one side and easier to withdraw if unscrewed. I have tried it. It does not work. The pliers is the best remedy.

If you do not have a pliers in the woods, use a couple of coins held between your thumb and index finger. If available, tincture of iodine, alcohol, or other disinfectant may be applied to reduce the danger of infection.

Dogs, of course, are notorious for acquiring a mouth and face full of quills. John Burroughs describes how his brother's farm collie, named Tige, kept chewing porcupines. Tige would yelp when each quill was pulled and then open his mouth for the next quill to be pulled.

Many dogs will whine and open their mouths after the last quill apparently has been pulled. It is well to wash out the dog's mouth and look again. Frequently a quill that has been missed, or one broken off in the tongue, will be found.

Various recommendations have been made for dequilling a dog. If it is large or greatly excited, the safest procedure is to stretch it around a tree with a rope attached to its collar. The rope is then pulled around the tree and tied around its body ahead of the hind legs. A stick can be placed in its mouth to keep it from biting.

Summer

Livestock are occasionally quilled by porcupines. Cattle usually get a muzzle full while smelling the porcupine out of curiosity. Cattle on the open range in mountainous country, where they are seldom looked at by ranchers in summer, can die of starvation after being struck with a hundred or more quills.

Horses are more inclined to kick at porcupines and thus receive quills in their legs and feet. The result may be stiff joints or deformities.

The profusion of summer in the aspen woods. This is porcupine country in western Colorado.

The World of the Porcupine

Domestic sheep are occasionally quilled when grazing on summer ranges. But vigilant herders usually find an animal that appears to be off feed or listless and soon remove the offending spines.

There is a published report from Nevada of a bighorn skull found with porcupine quills embedded in a small patch of skin remaining on the forehead. There was no certain evidence that the quills had killed the sheep.

The porcupine occasionally evens the score with his natural enemies. Coyotes, wolves, cougars, weasels, foxes, bears, eagles, and owls have been found with quills in their bodies. Undoubtedly these ene-

Porcupine in a gully high in the mountains in South Park, Colorado. They possibly eat the grass and shrub roots exposed by erosion as the gully banks wash away.

Porcupine in mountain meadow in northern Wyoming. Porcupines search for juicy herbs a mile or more from trees in areas like this at 8,000 to 9,000 feet elevation.

mies became victims of starvation when their mouths, eyes, or vital organs were pierced by a multitude of spines.

One enemy the porcupine has been unable to cope with is the automobile. Dead porcupines are a common sight along highways in forested areas. Some people have concluded that this is a sure sign of rapid increase in porcupine populations in recent years. Why not conclude that it is the result of increased numbers of automobiles? Porky, in its wanderings, doesn't have a chance when it crosses the road, now that we are adding seven or eight million new automobiles to the highways and byways each year. Also, we are annually building hundreds of

85

miles of new roads in the forests; so, Porky has more roads to cross in its wanderings.

Will a porcupine quill puncture an automobile tire? K. D. Flock states: "There is little doubt of this providing the barbed part of the quill gets well set into the fiber of the tire." But his report was published in 1934. Tires have changed since then. Also, the material in a tire is much tougher than the flesh of an animal or man and probably would not allow the scales of the quill to expand and retract with flexing as the tire revolves; thus the quill probably would not penetrate.

I have traveled on roads past numerous porcupines that have been flattened into the pavement by tires and have never encountered a motorist stopped by a puncture that could be attributed to quills. Quills in the composition soles of my boots have never worked through to my feet, even after months of tramping on trails, rocks, and in the woods. I believe that quills travel only through relatively soft materials like muscles of animals.

The porcupine's wandering undergoes a change in late summer. The beginnings of the sex urge, which will reach its culmination in autumn, initiate a wider range of exploration. The quest for food also changes since this is funeral time for much of the summer flora.

The tender grasses and succulent herbs of early season are gone. The wild onions, dandelions, geraniums, and dry-land sedges have dried and given place to purple ironweeds, goldenrods, tall sunflowers, and showy asters. Berries and bushes now offer a more tempting diet. The twigs of trees have stored much of their winter carbohydrates and next year's buds have been formed. In the transition to fall, the porcupine looks more frequently to its favorite trees for food.

Autumn

FALL IS AN UNQUIET TIME for the porcupine. The young have long been weaned from their mothers, and the reliable herbs of summer have died and been replaced by the ripening crops and fruits of autumn. Many edible things now are subject to the fickleness of weather. The increasing damage by morning frost, the colder air drainage in mountain glens, and the loss of concealing foliage from deciduous shrubs and trees transform the porcupine's world.

The porcupine feels the need to wander. There are new foods to be sampled, many to its liking. There are new shelters to be found, perhaps a vacant woods cabin, a hollow log, or the den among the boulders where generations of porcupines have rested before. And inwardly, a nervousness is beginning which will ultimately bring males and females together, for fall is the mating season.

If you want to see porcupines in autumn before the leaves drop, ride a horse. On a tall horse you are several feet higher than people on the ground. Also, on a horse, you are more likely to steer a course through tall shrubs and tree saplings than if you are walking. This puts you on eye-level with many porcupines that otherwise would never be seen.

I first became aware of porcupine sightings from the top of a horse in the San Miguel Mountains in southwestern Colorado. Much of this country, below the high mesa rims, is covered with almost impenetrable thickets of Gambel oak. With bullhide chaps you can navigate with a horse, if you stick to the labyrinth of cow trails in the brush. On a three-day ride through this country one fall, I saw five porcupines, all resting in the tops of oaks at heights of 6 to 8 feet above the ground. Without a horse, I would never walk any distance through this kind of country. But if I had walked, I probably would have seen no porcupines.

On a fall pack trip down **Saddle Creek**, which flows into the Snake River in Hell's Canyon between Oregon and Idaho, I saw two porcupines in willow clumps at eye-level. They would have been invisible to a man walking on the trail below the tree canopy. One of my companions wanted to shoot these porcupines, but I saved their lives by suggesting that the noise might "spook" the horses.

I remember sighting two other porcupines while riding a horse in tall shrubby vegetation on the Rampart Range north of Pikes Peak in Colorado one fall, and one near Cathedral Peak in northern Washington near the Canadian border.

I conclude from these and other similar experiences that porcupines find more concealment at medium heights in shrubs and small trees than most of us realize. They take advantage of any readily available cover when they are far from their favorite trees or dens during the fall migration.

The fall wanderings and migrations of porcupines in the East are usually localized. Their tracks can be seen more frequently on tote roads and in the sand in creek bottoms. But their cruising range is not greatly different from that of summer since their feeding areas are not greatly different from those a mile or even 10 miles away. The interspersion of summer and winter food makes migration unnecessary.

Drifts of porcupine populations and migrations of individuals are more common in the West, particularly in regions where the combination of deserts, foothills, and mountains present drastically different habitats at different seasons. The travel-ways followed by western porcupines in autumn have one characteristic in common—they lead to trees and terrain which will provide food and shelter during the coming winter.

These two needs, food and shelter, seem to have more influence on seasonal drift of porcupines than altitudinal change or severity of weather. In the Pacific Northwest, where I have studied many porcupines, I find them going both up and down the mountains in autumn.

In the high Wallowa Mountains of eastern Oregon, the porcupines migrate down from the alpine meadows into spruce-fir forests. In the Blue Mountains, the numerous porcupines in the low elevation meadows tend to drift higher into the pine zone, and when winter comes they are most likely to be found within short distances from rocky dens. On the other hand, the porcupines in the Steens Mountains make their autumn trek downward from the sagebrush-grass ranges to the cottonwood and willow groves along the river courses where winter food is abundant. In southern Idaho the migration is upward from the sagebrush borders into the pine and spruce zones.

The most remarkable porcupine migration on record is that written by William T. Cox and quoted by Walter P. Taylor. In the autumn of

Porcupines in autumn occasionally eat shaggy-mane mushrooms.

Porcupine food—mushrooms.

The World of the Porcupine

1907, Cox and others were crossing the Rocky Mountains in northern Montana when they noticed streaks in the snow in the distant gaps and saddles between the mountain peaks. The party traveled on snowshoes for several miles to investigate and found hundreds of porcupines migrating westward.

The porcupines, according to Cox, were going into well-timbered country and warmer territory than prevailed east of the mountains. He speculated that it might have been one of those migrations in which a whole body of animals moves to new territory to find by chance more favorable environment for propagation and persistence of the species. There is no record that this type of migration is repeated yearly in the locality observed by Cox.

In late autumn and winter, wherever the porcupine may be, the main source of food is the inner bark of trees. On young trees the stem may be almost completely stripped. The tops of larger trees may be girdled. In other instances, patches of bark a square foot or more in area may be removed.

In the Northeast and in some of the Canadian provinces, hemlock and sugar maple are favorite porcupine foods. In New Brunswick, W. A. Reeks lists the following favorite trees: spruce, pine, larch, fir, birch, beech, and poplar. He points out that first choice for any given locality is probably determined by relative abundance of the various tree species.

In Pennsylvania and elsewhere it has been observed that porcupines commonly confine their feeding on beech to the base of the tree. Reeks states that the trees are usually chewed only on one side and are seldom girdled or attacked farther up the stem or in the branches. He suggests that the bark is thin enough at the base to provide satisfactory food without climbing. I believe also that the smooth bark of the beech makes climbing difficult; hence the porcupine is content to feed at the ground level.

In the North Central states, porcupines feast in the fall on acorns, beechnuts, or corn, if it is available. They are fond of apples and will

90

Baby porcupines eat fruits and vegetables at an early age.

make use of fall vegetable crops, including turnips, if they are available. Carrots also are relished by porcupines.

The proportion of nuts, fruits, and other ground-gathered food rapidly diminishes as fall progresses through September and October. By the end of November the food of the animal is almost exclusively tree-gathered.

Not all the tree-gathered food of western porcupines is bark. Pine needles are eaten regularly as are late-growing mushrooms. Mistletoe is a preferred food, but the porcupine is probably ineffective in its control. As Taylor states, "We do not know whether the porcupine came first and brought the mistletoe or the mistletoe came first and attracted the porcupine."

The variety and availability of edible things is shown by a list of foods found acceptable by Nevada porcupines. In September, choke-

91

cherries, acorns, and piñon nuts are in season. So are rose leaves, serviceberry leaves and bark, and alfalfa in the fields. Goldenrods, asters, rabbit brush, and late-blooming dandelions also appear in profusion. All of these are eaten by porcupines.

Other favorite foods that have been listed for porcupines in Nevada include the bark of whitebark pine, Douglas fir, Fremont cottonwood, and curl-leaf mountain mahogany. Geranium, sedge, mountain bluebells, and knotweed, including both stems and seeds, are eaten before frost kills these succulent herbs.

Along with changes in food habits, changes in the porcupine itself occur in fall. The short underfur that has been absent in summer begins to grow and thicken. In northern areas where winters are exceptionally severe, it will be almost as dense as the fleece on a sheep. I have parted this "wool" on gentle porcupines with my fingers and found the fibers to be more than an inch in length. No wonder they can endure temperatures far below zero.

In early fall, or even in late summer, other more subtle changes occur in the porcupine. The males become restless and travel more in their territories. When they encounter one another they go through the motions of fighting but never actually engage in battle. They also ride sticks and even sit upright holding them in their paws.

The females indulge in similar activities, accompanied by crooning or whining sounds which sometimes are answered by the males in louder tones. Both sexes gnaw sticks, tin cans, and other inedible objects, more as a means of making noise, I believe, than as a search for food.

In this respect my friend John Clouston described one of his experiences in eastern Oregon. He was awakened from a sound sleep at a ranger station by an intermittent booming that came from the horse barn. "It sounded exactly like someone playing a bull fiddle," he said. When he had dressed and was warily approaching the barn, the "boom . . . boom . . . boom" still continued. The light from his lantern finally revealed the cause—a large porcupine gnawing the extended portion of a board that was nailed only at one end to the building. The reverberations were being produced each time the porcupine applied his teeth to the "sounding board".

The building of the sex urge is manifested in many ways over a period of several weeks. This is the courtship of the porcupine. Observations of its varied phases by woodsmen and others have led to many legends and ridiculous interpretations of their breeding habits.

Porcupine reproductive activities have been studied scientifically by competent observers. Young females do not breed until they are at least one year of age since mature ovarian activity does not begin

Porcupine food—geranium in the Blue Mountains of Oregon.

before that time. Ovulation begins at about the age of one and one-half years. The estrual, or "heat," period ranges over several months, particularly from September through December. The cycle is repeated each 25 or 30 days if breeding does not occur. This may explain the different ages and sizes of young porcupines found in the woods during the following spring and summer. Most females produce young in their second and third years. The percentage of successful births is high.

The World of the Porcupine

Several weeks before the mating season, the females show evidence of nervousness and greater excitability. Young females are more active than usual, exercise vigorously, and even run without provocation from outside stimuli. They gnaw various objects without eating them. And more frequently than usual they chatter their teeth, moan, or even emit eerie sobbing cries. Older females are less inclined to nervousness and excitement.

When porcupines meet at this time they check the odors of one another. Sometimes they rub noses. Observations of porcupines sitting upright face to face, sometimes with their forepaws touching, have resulted in the speculation that this is the culmination of their courtship. Actually, these activities are only manifestations of the long emotional and physiological preparation for the time when the female will receive the male essentially in the manner common to mammalian quadrupeds.

Male porcupines at the approach of the mating season travel more than usual and are inclined to whine in louder tones. If they encounter other males, they may appear to fight, but only momentarily. Usually they continue their search for females, following scent marks and listening for their cries.

Males and females may remain together for some days before mating. They may touch paws and even walk on their hind feet in the so-called love dance of the porcupine. The female accepts the male only when she is ready. Coupling may be repeated during a period of several hours, and then she goes her separate way.

Few people have witnessed the actual copulation of the porcupine. P. H. Struthers witnessed it once in the laboratory, and Walter P. Taylor summarized the information known up to 1935. The process is de-

Defense posture of porcupine—head hidden, all quills erect.

The "irritable back" of the porcupine with several thousand spines erected for protection.

Porcupine killed by automobile. These casualties nearly always occur at night.

scribed in considerable detail by Albert R. Shadle in the April, 1946, *Journal of Wildlife Management.* Photographs confirming the observations are included in the article.

One of the female porcupines observed by Dr. Shadle showed signs of rut for three or four weeks before the peak of heat was reached. A male porcupine in the adjoining half of her cage made frequent olfactory tests which made him more or less sexually excited. He evidenced this excitement in various ways, including whining, doing a three-legged walk, and rubbing his nose against objects.

Mating was accomplished in the two cases described with the female standing on all four feet and the male standing erect, using his hind legs and tail for support. The male did not use his fore limbs to hold the female.

Although the gestation period is seven months or more, and porcupine births are single, populations sometimes build up to exceptional numbers in local areas. Peaks in population cycles have been recorded in some localities at 10- to 20-year intervals.

These peaks in population numbers are generally accompanied by a rash of newspaper reports and some reports in the forestry literature. Most of the censuses on which these reports are based are taken haphazardly at best, usually in conjunction with a timber cruising project. Counts on small areas where porcupines have congregated near winter dens are extrapolated to thousands of acres or even hundreds of square miles. Thus the erroneous impression is given that porcupines are evenly distributed in large numbers over an entire forest or even part of a state.

One census, made in an area of 1½ square miles in northern Minnesota, served as the basis for an estimate that a 35-square-mile area had a population of 1,600 porcupines! No indication was given in the report that the other 33½ square miles had been searched for porcupines. A report from Wisconsin cites a population of 1.9 porcupines per acre, based on kill records added together for May and October for a small local area.

Local concentrations of porcupines do occur. Donald Spencer states that the owner of a small apple orchard in Maine trapped sixty-five porcupines at harvest time one fall. I saw seven porcupines at one time around my camp at the edge of Bryce Canyon in Utah. Although I roamed the vicinity for several days and camped in three other locations, I never saw another porcupine.

One can find in the literature almost any estimate he wants. For the specific areas described, the reports probably are reliable within the limits of the sampling method used.

The variation among published reports is wide. Taylor reported three to fifteen porcupines per square mile in Arizona and New Mexico. On the basis of a hunter "sight survey," Frank B. Golley estimated two per square mile for the entire Upper Peninsula of Michigan. One was reported for every 26 acres in Wisconsin. Shapiro estimated one for each 52 acres in New York. Reeks estimated six to eight per

Much of the dense underfur is lost during the summer molt. Some of the fur is being shed at the back and at the base of the tail, exposing the spines even when the animal is in repose.

square mile in New Brunswick. Curtis reported ten to fourteen per square mile in red spruce forests in Maine.

In working up the photographic material for this book, I have come to appreciate the difficulty of finding porcupines when I want them. Recently I traveled over 2,500 miles running down reports of porcupine concentrations in Oregon and Washington. The trips always ended in failure—no one was able to show me a porcupine where porcupines were reported to be in epidemic numbers.

The explanations varied. One comment was, "Maybe they've all been shot or poisoned." Another was, "They were numerous when we camped here three years ago." Still another was, "I know there are porcupines here. One got into my tent when I camped at this very spot

98

A rock den in the northern Cascade Mountains.

in 1959." One woodsman said, "Look at the porcupine scars on the trees. They're everywhere." When I looked at the scars I found that they were anywhere from two to ten years old.

For a better understanding of porcupine scars and porcupine numbers, I recommend a reading of Donald A. Spencer's fascinating study of porcupine population fluctuations in past centuries on the Mesa Verde National Park. In company with Herbert A. Schwan, I explored this area in 1946, about the time the study was started. The porcupine eruption was a serious one, and the piñon pines showed much evidence of porcupine use.

Spencer's description of the appearance of feeding scars on piñon pine at different periods following the removal of bark and phloem is excellent. Feeding that has occurred within the past twenty-four hours leaves a gleaming white wood surface on which no resin exudate is visible.

He states: "In the following 48 h, tiny crystalline-clear drops of resinous sap begin to dot the surface. This 72 h picture very slowly changes until by the second week after tree injury, the clear tacky drops are $\frac{1}{4}$ in. in diameter as the result of growth and coalescence.

99

Porcupine country in central Oregon.

Progressively, the drops of clear pitch begin to sag and then run in long streamers down the trunk of the tree, a characteristic condition up to 4 months after scar formation. The slightly off-white appearance of the scar identifies it throughout the first fall-winter season. The second and third year after scar formation the pitch covering the wound still has tacky components and is a distinct yellow. In a period of 3-10 years (depending upon the position of the scar with respect to wind and weathering) the yellow resin which at first forms a continuous hard protective coat over the wound is weathered away into chalky, yellowish patches. During this same interval large, hard globes of resin form about the perimeter of the wound, which in time, are likewise lost. The earthy, dead-wood surface that follows loss of the resin protective coat is at first hard and of smooth contour, but gradually is attacked by fungi and weather to assume a fine, linear-ridged appearance, often broken here and there by the holes of wood-burrowing insects."

Other tree species react differently to porcupine feeding than the piñon pine. Ponderosa pines, oaks, and elms, for example, cover the scars with bark in a few years. Maple trees sometimes produce a large swelling at the top of the scar due to the downward flow of sugar and other substances. The implication is clear. If one wishes to estimate

100

porcupine populations by the kind and number of feeding scars on trees, careful records of age and appearance of the scars should be kept.

Spencer's study combined the intriguing method of dating tree rings back through the centuries with the incidence of porcupine damage as shown by feeding scars. He states: "Fortunately for this investigation into animal fluctuations over the past 200-250 years, piñon pine makes a growth response to a wound that is almost perfectly designed to perpetuate the dendrochronologic record. In the first place, the piñon never succeeds in obliterating a wound by the in-rolling of new wood from the perimeter. For example, a scar showing the date of the year 1693 had less than ½ in. about the perimeter covered with new growth. Secondly, sufficient 'over-rolling' of the new wood about the

A beaver's chewing job. Porcupines eat only the bark.

101

Porcupine in a dead alligator juniper in Arizona.

perimeter, that preserves the outermost xylem ring of the scar from subsequent weathering away, occurs during the first 10 years when the scar face has its initial resin shield."

Spencer found that over a period of 120 years porcupine eruptions occurred during four periods with greatest animal abundance centered about the years 1845, 1885, 1905, and 1935. Over the previous period, 1690 to 1835, fewer scars were found for the study. But they formed four groups indicating that the peaks of eruptions occurred in the years 1716, 1745, 1785, and 1815.

The rise and decline of these population eruptions covered periods of twelve to twenty years, indicating that porcupines, with their single young per year, require considerable time to reach a peak in numbers. Spencer also found "an interval of approximately 10 years between the termination of one population surge and the beginning of another, during which periods porcupines are extremely scarce. . . ."

The scarcest porcupines of all are the albinos. Albinism is the condition in which color pigmentation is absent. When yellow and black

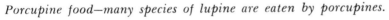

Porcupine food—many species of lupine are eaten by porcupines.

103

pigment is lacking, the animal has creamy white skin and white hair. The eyes are pink due to the blood circulating in minute vessels which show its color because of the lack of pigmentation. It has been estimated that about one in 50,000 porcupines is an albino.

Many years ago George Shiras watched and photographed an albino porcupine over a period of six years near Whitefish Lake east of Marquette, Michigan. Every part of the animal except the eyes was white, including the quills, hair, claws, and nose. The eyes were bright translucent pink in sunlight.

This porcupine was deaf and blind. It was indifferent to photographic flash and to the sound of voices, but the scent of people caused it to take instant alarm. It consistently used the same well-worn path between its den and the lake shore where it always fed down-wind.

Probably the most famous albino porcupine was the one obtained by Caesarean section by Donald A. Spencer near Carthage, New York, in 1941. "Pinkie" was turned over to Dr. Albert R. Shadle at the University of Buffalo where it grew to a weight of 25 pounds. It was used in numerous scientific experiments and twice traveled across the United States making public appearances. It looked like any normal porcupine, except for its lack of color, when it was photographed at the age of nine years.

Another albino porcupine was discovered in an apple tree by Guy W. Tucker in November, 1955, in Maine. "Snowball" became an impractical pet, so Tucker shipped it to Boston's Museum of Science where it became an interesting attraction at Science Park.

Recently, I spent several days and traveled several hundred miles in an attempt to locate an alleged albino porcupine in southern Oregon. An employee of the State of Oregon had been told that the proprietor of a gem shop in Lakeview owned a pet albino. The gem shop owner told me that, though he did not own a white porcupine, he had seen pictures of one in the newspaper published in Klamath Falls about two years before my visit.

Autumn

The Klamath Falls newspaper had no porcupine pictures in the photo morgue but the editor suggested I contact an insurance salesman who had a hobby of giving nature lectures. The salesman had never heard of the albino porcupine, but he knew a lady who kept pets at one time near Quartz Mountain, which is in the hills between Klamath Falls and Lakeview. The lady had never had a pet albino, but the people at Quartz Mountain had seen a picture of one in the Portland *Oregonian*.

At the *Oregonian* they said, "Yes, we have a picture of an albino." When I looked at the print, there was Dr. Shadle's white porcupine from Buffalo, New York. It had been widely publicized by the Associated Press.

I have found no report of an albino porcupine ever being seen by a hunter. This seems odd since several million hunters take to the woods each fall during the deer and elk seasons. Across the nation, they see thousands of porcupines.

A survey of porcupine sightings among deer hunters, reported by Frank B. Golley, provides data for some intriguing speculations. In the Upper Peninsula of Michigan in 1955, the 1,060 deer hunters interviewed had seen 309 porcupines and killed only 29. On this basis it was estimated that the total of 115,110 hunters killed between 2,520 and 4,640 porcupines and saw between 31,100 and 40,300. The report makes no mention of an albino porcupine being seen. But even more interesting is the finding that hunters killed less than one out of every ten porcupines seen.

Bark eaten from sagebrush, Artemisia cana, by mice on Grand Mesa at 10,000-foot elevation in western Colorado. Porcupines leave larger teeth marks which are parallel instead of being scattered as in mouse nibbling.

105

The World of the Porcupine

I suspect that some hunters do not kill porcupines because the sound of the shot might scare the game they are pursuing. Others enjoy the porcupine as an interesting creature of the woods and as one of the worth-while memories of their experience in the wilds. Some probably believe that porcupines should be left as an easy source of food for people lost in the wilderness.

In my own experience during the fall hunting seasons in the West, porcupines are not often seen because of various circumstances. The breeding season is in progress, and porcupines do most of their wandering at night. If they are sleeping in trees in the daytime, they are not likely to be seen since big game hunters confine their attention to places beneath the trees where game may be found.

As autumn ends, porcupines begin to establish paths and travel-ways between favorite feeding trees and winter dens. Some forsake their solitary habits and live with other porcupines in the same shelters when winter comes to the forest.

Winter

UNLIKE BEARS, CHIPMUNKS, AND MARMOTS, porcupines do not hibernate. They do seek shelter during stormy weather, although they can endure extremely low temperatures without apparent discomfort. I believe that some dens are used more to escape wet weather than to protect the animals from subzero weather.

Jacob Shapiro, however, states that "dryness does not appear to be an important factor in den choice in the Adirondacks, as three dens on the shores of lakes near swamps were not particularly dry." In support of this opinion, I have seen porcupines enter wet dens with standing water in the entrances in the Douglas fir region in western Washington. I do not believe the water underfoot bothers them as much as prolonged heavy winter rain which soaks their underfur to the skin. When they have a choice between dry and wet dens, they almost invariably use the dry ones.

Porcupines will enter holes in the ground such as badger and coyote dens if the hole is large enough. The porcupines I have observed using these holes can emerge backward without difficulty by relaxing their quills.

I have been in porcupine dens in rock caves and abandoned mines where it was possible for a man to stand erect. In others, the space between the rock layers was less than a foot from floor to ceiling, but it was sufficient for free movement of the animals.

107

The World of the Porcupine

Old abandoned houses and barns are occasionally used for shelter. Sometimes porcupines are found living beneath the floors of occupied dwellings. I know of one porcupine that used a crevice in a stone fence for shelter.

Dens are usually close to the food supply. Those used occasionally in summer and fall are likely to be found near orchards, alfalfa fields, melon patches, or vegetable gardens. Those used in winter are nearly always in the forest or close to groups of trees that will supply the bark for the winter diet.

The mere presence of dens does not mean that porcupines will be in them. Large numbers of porcupines spend weeks and even months in trees during periods of deep snow. One of these, near Ogden, Utah, ate most of the bark of a 60-foot ponderosa pine tree from the top down for a distance of 20 feet. It left its station after remaining in the tree through January, February, and March. A suitable den was not available within reasonable traveling distance from its food tree.

Porcupines transport no padding for the beds in their dens. Dens used year after year accumulate a deep layer of pellets which disintegrate very slowly if the place is dry. Ultimately this layer fills the crevices of the rocks, and the activities of the porcupines smooth it to a comparatively level floor. When dens are used by generation after generation of porcupines, the pellet layer sometimes accumulates to a depth of several feet.

My friend, Burt R. McConnell, recently attempted to show me a

Gentian flowers are eaten by porcupines above timber line in high mountain areas.

Porcupine enemy. Weasel caught in trap set for gophers on Grand Mesa in western Colorado. Weasels have been reported as porcupine killers in various parts of the country.

Fisher, the porcupine's most efficient enemy in nature.

OREGON GAME COMMISSION

most remarkable den near Twisp, Washington. I failed to see it because we were turned back by deep snow. In describing the den, Burt stated that the pellets had accumulated to such an extent that they had cascaded from the den opening down a steep slope for many yards.

Porcupines appear to show no marked preference as to den exposure. Most of those I have seen have been about equally divided between east, south, and west exposures. I can remember seeing only a few dens with north exposure. This may be the result of snow obstructing the entrances to otherwise favorable places on north slopes.

109

Porcupine food—Alpine blue-grass, Poa alpina, *found in high Western mountains.*

Runways from winter dens are particularly useful for determining the winter cruising radius of porcupines. These runs are easily identified by the pigeon-toed tracks and the tail marks in fresh snow. Feeding runs extend from a few feet to one-fourth mile or more. They seldom average more than three or four hundred feet in length in places where trees and dens are close together.

Pellets or scats are invariably present beneath feeding trees. A sharp observer may use these to locate porcupines in trees that are so densely covered with foliage as to otherwise obscure the animals or their work.

Shapiro believes that the animal voids three times a day, based on observation of ice formed about pellets and on markings in the snow. In their dens, porcupines certainly are not good housekeepers. The odor of urine permeates their habitations and announces the presence of dens to humans who have a good sense of smell.

Various studies indicate that porcupines evacuate from 75 to 200 pellets per day. Pellets in winter resemble little oval sawdust bri-quettes which are gray or yellow, depending somewhat on the species

110

Baby porcupines love milk but have poor table manners.

of tree on which the animal feeds. Sometimes the pellets are joined together like sausage links.

If a pellet is crushed it will be seen to consist mainly of wood fibers indicating a fine job of chewing. One study has reported that the porcupine masticates as much as twelve times between bites. I checked this on my last pet porcupine and found that it chewed from seven to sixteen times between each bite while eating carrots.

Close observation of a porcupine in the woods will demonstrate that it spends considerable time smelling things other than food. When a full-grown male is introduced into a cage, he thoroughly examines every part and every object with his nose. He pays particular attention to places where other porcupines have urinated.

Porcupines are attracted by the odor of urine of other animals and man. This may explain the basis for reports of porcupines chewing on automobile tires which are regularly urinated on by dogs. Instances of porcupines chewing toilet seats in camp grounds are exceedingly numerous.

Injury to woody plants is sometimes erroneously ascribed to the porcupine. Each animal leaves its characteristic mark and close examination will usually give a clue to the proper animal. Large animals such as elk, deer, cattle, sheep, and goats break trees and shrubs, pull off bark in long narrow strips, or at least leave ragged broken ends on twigs and small branches. Bear, lynx, and bobcat damage usually shows claw marks and sometimes large pieces of bark scattered on the ground.

Beavers make slanting tooth marks and cut down entire trees. Porcupines make clean slanting cuts up to ¾ inch in diameter on branches and twigs. They remove patches of bark of various sizes from trees anywhere from the base to the top. Mice, squirrels, and other rodents girdle and chew twigs and branches in various ways, but their tooth marks are smaller than those left by the porcupine.

Five-day-old porcupine that was delivered by Caesarean section.

112

The World of the Porcupine

The porcupine's teeth are remarkably adapted for the chewing he has to do in his lifetime of eight to ten years. The dental formula is: $i. \frac{1}{1}, pm. \frac{1}{1}, m. \frac{3}{3}$. This means, for one side of the animal's mouth, one incisor above and one below; one premolar above and one below; and three molars above and three below. The teeth on two sides add up to twenty.

The incisors have yellow- or orange-colored enamel and are from .09 to .14 inch in width. By comparison, the incisors of beavers are about .24 inch in width while those of the meadow mouse are about .06 inch. The incisors of porcupines continue to grow throughout life.

In young porcupines the last molars are not erupted at birth, so the baby porcupine starts life with eight teeth. In adults, the molars are large and flat crowned. These large molars are well adapted for masticating bark, wood, and other hard substances so commonly found in the diet of the porcupine.

In the Northeast, porcupines sometimes chew the plastic hoses used to collect sap for maple syrup. Other objects for which chewing has been reported include: cork handles of fishing rods, harness, saddles, road signs, canoe paddles, aluminum pails, leather boots, camp tables, and smoke houses. But from the forester's viewpoint, the porcupine's greatest liability is its winter diet of evergreen needles and the bark of trees.

The winter eating habits of porcupines vary according to the availability of food, the weather, and the nearness to dens. When snow is deep, porcupines sometimes gnaw patches of wood from small- and middle-sized trees at the snow line. If the injury is extensive, it affects' the butt log which is the most valuable part of the tree.

If dens are not near, porcupines may remain in trees for long periods. Then they are apt to girdle the stems, causing the tree tops to die. Some "spike top" trees, however, are blamed on porcupines when actually the damage was caused by lightning, insects, fungi, or wind breakage.

114

Winter

Porcupines sometimes confine their feeding to certain groups of trees with the result that nearly every tree in an area of one-fourth acre or more may show some damage. Between these local damage areas there may be little evidence of feeding for several miles.

It has been reported for parts of Oregon that a third of the second-growth lodgepole pine timber has been damaged. The report does not state what parts of Oregon, or how big those parts were. To give the porcupine its due, foresters should be specific about location, size of area, and method of sampling used in estimating damage.

Before releasing statistics that blame the porcupine for tree losses on plantations, a correct determination should be made of the amount of loss caused by deer, rabbits, drought, damping-off fungi, insects, lethal soil temperatures, and herbaceous plant competition.

Taylor has discussed porcupine damage in the Southwest at length in his monographic study published by the University of Arizona. He states: "Ordinarily, it is impracticable, even for an experienced observer, to estimate fairly the amount and seriousness of porcupine work in a forest of varying character by simply traveling through it. Deliberate examination of trees of all classes, under different conditions ... is necessary." He concluded: "Certainly the greater part of the forest area in the Southwest is in no danger from porcupines."

In an interesting study of porcupine food preferences in Minnesota, Paul O. Rudolf observed that Scotch pines of central European origin suffered more damage than those that came from northern Europe. Further consideration of the data, however, indicated that the choice was based more on tree size than on source of tree seed. In his study area, porcupines preferred trees at least 3 inches in diameter (at breast height) and 14 feet high. He suggested that smaller trees provide less bark for food, less security while feeding, and are more difficult to climb.

James D. Curtis states: "Porcupines often return year after year to the same tree. About half the time they increase the size of the original

115

Porcupine raiding a garden on a farm at night.

scar rather than choose other parts of the stem. This is common on sugar maple and hemlock.''

The generally accepted explanation is that the feeding scar stops the downward flow of sugar in the bark. Porcupines have learned that the accumulated sweetness is preferable to unused parts of the tree.

A porcupine never starves, if it is in good health and has no physical injury. It makes sure that it has bark to eat in winter. And in summer it has all the plants of forest, meadow, and field to eat. In addition to its staple foods—bark, shrubs, leaves, and herbs—it is attracted by exotic odors and substances, including glue in plywood boards. Almost anything that has been touched by human hands, or that has become salt-impregnated by cooking, or by smoking of meat or fish, is a temptation for porcupines to chew.

One cabin owner solved the problem of porcupines chewing on his house in the woods by building a wooden platform in the yard. Salt placed on the boards melted in the rain and seeped down through the wood. Each winter thereafter the porcupines chewed the boards and never bothered the cabin.

Craving for salt has led to the destruction of many porcupines in the past. Blocks of wood with a salt-strychnine mixture in auger holes were placed in dens or nailed to trees above the reach of livestock. I once saw five porcupine carcasses beneath a baited tree near Ephraim, Utah, where no possibility of timber cutting existed. Taylor has mentioned the risk to tree squirrels, mantled ground squirrels, chipmunks, and jays in using poison blocks in trees.

Porcupines occasionally perform a service for deer and rabbits by clipping twigs and branches that are inaccessible to wild life when snow is deep and ground level browse is scarce. In late fall, branches of oak and beech are sometimes clipped to obtain acorns and beechnuts. Many of these fall to the ground and are available to non-climbing animals.

Branches that obstruct the porcupine's progress in the tree sometimes are clipped with a few rapid bites. These fall to the ground where other grazing animals can eat them.

118

Winter

Porcupines are not sufficiently numerous in the West to reduce the occasional winter starvation of deer by providing clipped branches of pine, spruce, and fir. Although I have seen areas in Oregon and Washington where the snow was liberally strewn with dropped foliage of Douglas fir, the amount was insufficient to prevent the deaths of hundreds of deer that were unable to find enough feed in the deep snow.

The porcupine is not bothered by deep snow. If you follow its pigeon-toed tracks and the tail-drag marks, its apparent aimless wandering eventually will lead either to a den where it waits out the severe storms or to a tree where it may gnaw bark for days on end.

Snow can be a help to porcupines. They can walk on it, and as it builds higher they can reach inaccessible twigs and other food. One can sometimes note the slanting cuts on stems of bushes that are too slender to sustain the animal's weight in snowless seasons.

One winter the snow enabled the porcupines to widen all the joints on the siding of a cook house near Toll Gate in eastern Oregon. As the "white platform" accumulated during the winter, they chewed higher and higher until by spring every crack between the boards had been widened as though done with a carpenter's routing tool.

Alpine country. Porcupines occasionally wander up to the meadows at 12,000 feet or more in the Colorado Rocky Mountains when the showy plants are in bloom.

The World of the Porcupine

Snow also can hamper the porcupine's movements. When it is soft and fluffy, their waddling from dens to trees is impeded, and they tend to concentrate their food gathering in nearby feeding areas. In time, if the snow does not continue to accumulate or to drift, their trails become packed and sometimes are less likely to melt than the rest of the snow. These winter trails are still used after the late winter thaws.

I remember a visit to Cameron Pass in the Colorado Rockies in a "snow cat" to measure the stored moisture at 10,000 feet. One of my companions was puzzled by tracks that crossed the space between dense stands of spruce. "What makes a track with a line in the middle?" he asked. The other companion answered, "A raccoon dragging something."

On closer examination, I recognized the footprints of a porcupine. Although we put on our snowshoes, we were unable to follow the trail among the dense branches of the spruce trees which were buried 15 feet in high-altitude winter snow.

The porcupine's ability to live at high altitude in winter was demonstrated to me many years ago on the Wasatch Plateau in Utah. On an early spring trip several of us climbed on snowshoes to the 10,000-foot level. The sun was shining brightly, and the temperature was nearly 70 degrees. Every animal of the mountain top seemed to be abroad. The snow was plastered with marmots, ground squirrels, and gophers. Hawks were everywhere, but they were unable to catch the rodents who could dive into the innumerable holes they had dug up through ten feet of snow.

We used the opportunity to study a multitude of animal tracks and identify them with their makers. But we were puzzled by larger tracks than those made by any of the visible animals. Mostly, these larger tracks were at the edge of timber which filled the ravines. Years later, the riddle was solved when I saw the animal that left these footprints —my old friend the porcupine.

The porcupine has another adaptation which I believe aids it in its rugged winter life. It has a large liver which possibly stores needed

120

vitamin and other substances during the fall abundance of fat-producing foods such as acorns, beechnuts, corn, and fruits of shrubs and trees. These stored substances certainly would tend to balance deficiencies in the unchanging winter diet of cambium and phloem from the inner bark of trees.

The porcupine undoubtedly is innately aware that its diet cannot be changed by searching for ground-layer vegetation in deep winter. So it remains in its tree even though the storms shake it to the root and the snow obscures the bark on the windward side of its table.

But when the thaw takes the snow, the porcupine is gone from its tree. Soon the sap will be rising in more succulent browse, and there will be new foods to sample. The female porcupines, with developing young in their bodies, also have need for varied diets. Hence, with the approach of spring, porcupines increase their wandering or begin the slow migrations that will take them to their summer homes.

With the coming of spring, porcupine damage to trees decreases. But the scars caused by their winter feeding remain and become the primary cause for porcupine control programs. Various control methods have been tried, including shooting, trapping, hunting with dogs, the bounty system, and poisoned baits.

The bounty system has been used for many years to control porcupines. Since the early 1900's porcupine bounties have amounted to more than $162,300 in Vermont and $165,000 in Maine. Some hunters in Vermont fashioned as many as sixteen pairs of ears from the underparts of one porcupine skin. A recent *State Guide to Varmint Hunting*, by Pete Brown, states that bounties on porcupines are still paid in New Hampshire and in some counties in New York. In spite of this outmoded system, porcupines continue to thrive.

The bounty system has been abandoned by most states for predator as well as porcupine control. The bounty hunter frequently uses fraudulent practices, including "leaving some animals for seed," collecting fees for animals trapped outside the bounty or damage area, and passing off ears or other evidence from other animals to unwary bounty officials who do not know the difference between a badger foot and a porcupine foot, or between a coyote ear and a bobcat ear.

Porcupine control is practiced on a hit-and-miss basis by ranchers who occasionally find a cow or horse that has been quilled. They usually do not systematically hunt porcupines but merely kill those that are sighted on their livestock or range inspection trips. In mountainous country these trips are usually made in summer when livestock are on the range, and porcupines are difficult to locate because of dense foliage on trees and rank growth of herbaceous plants on the ground.

Hunters have been hired to control porcupines by shooting them when damage to tree plantations appears excessive. This is an expensive practice and not always a productive one. Many porcupines are never seen even though the hunter systematically covers a given territory. Best success occurs in winter when shooting is done in porcupine concentration areas.

Revolvers or .22 rifles are generally used by porcupine hunters. Some weird tales have come from hunters and others with regard to the amount of "lead" a porcupine can take before it is killed. I am inclined to believe that many of these tales are exaggerations or a "cover-up" for some poor shooting. One porcupine that I saw skinned after being shot "a dozen times" showed only one hole, the one caused by the bullet that killed him. The other bullets may have passed through the quills without touching the body, which is a deceptively small target in a tall tree at a distance of 50 yards or more.

I consider a .22 revolver inhumane for killing porcupines at long distances. The bullet simply does not have the foot-pounds of energy

Winter den in rocks in Cascade Mountains of central Oregon. Author in picture.

Porcupines prefer to travel on snow that has crusted slightly; if it is soft and deep, they stay in dens and trees.

necessary to blast the animal into eternity as would a high-powered rifle.

Trapping for porcupine control is seldom used except for animals that are found living under farm buildings or are found repeatedly doing damage to cabins- or other structures. Porcupines also are trapped at the entrances to their dens where they are reasonably certain to follow a path in which the trap is placed. Trappers sometimes are annoyed by porcupines blundering into sets made for coyotes, foxes, martins, or other fur bearers. The scent used on the bait attracts porcupines.

The most effective control method involves the use of poisoned bait placed either in trees or in dens. In the past, the porcupine's fondness for salt has been used as the basis for poison methods. Poison consisting of one ounce of powdered strychnine to one pound of table salt was placed in dens or on ledges frequented by porcupines. One tablespoon to a bait was sufficient. In arid regions, water or magnesium carbonate was added to the poison mixture to cause caking and thus prevent the bait's being blown away by the wind.

In areas where rock dens did not exist or where summer poisoning was desired, the poison mixture was poured into auger holes or gouged-out cavities in blocks of wood. These blocks were nailed to trees out of reach of cattle and deer and 6 to 8 inches above a limb on which the porcupine could sit while eating the poison mixture. The

123

salt-strychnine combination was generally stirred into vegetable cooking fat which kept the poison in the wood block during stormy periods.

A method of control widely employed in Vermont involves the use of sodium arsenite mixed with granulated sugar. The mixture is poured into cone-shaped holes cut in ripe apples. The plugs removed from the apples are replaced after the poison has been inserted.

A few apples are placed in each porcupine den. The authors of the method, Clarence E. Faulkner and Wendell E. Dodge, state: "The

Branch cut from tall fir by porcupine. In winter these cuttings are browsed by deer and rabbits.

apples are placed well back in the dens where other species of animals are not nearly so likely to encounter them as are the porcupines. . . . The dangers of secondary poisoning also are not great, since the porcupines invariably die in the den and are relatively inaccessible to other forms" of wild life.

An occasional dog will learn the trick of barking "treed" when it locates a porcupine. Many years ago Walter P. Taylor described such a dog in *American Forestry*. He called the animal, "Four Thousand Dollar Dog."

I have known only two dogs that barked "treed" when they located porcupines. One was a beagle that belonged to Richard S. Driscoll in Bend, Oregon. The other was a coon dog of uncertain breed and kidney that belonged to a farmer near Sauk City, Wisconsin.

124

Winter presents no food problem to the porcupine in the forest. Trees provide both food and shelter.

Dick Driscoll's dog, Sam, once encountered a porcupine near Thompson Reservoir in southern Oregon when I was present. The porcupine was waddling across a meadow about 100 yards from the nearest tree when Sam charged up to it with all the screeching and yodeling of which a beagle is capable. My first thought was, "Here's where we get a dog full of quills."

The porcupine, immediately aware of the attack, stiffened its legs, raised its body, and erected all quills. Although its head was held low to the ground it always whirled to present a prickly rear to the dog. The porcupine struck several times with its tail, but Sam was always at a safe distance behind or was attempting to charge at the head end of the porcupine.

The dog never made contact with the porcupine. Instead, he stopped frequently and looked at his master with such a quizzical expression that we both howled with laughter. Sam didn't quite know what to do with the creature that lurched from side to side and spun around so quickly. When we finally allowed the porcupine to climb a pine tree, Sam lustily barked "treed" for a minute or two.

The Wisconsin episode happened on a dark night in the Baraboo Hills. The five dogs with the party spent the first couple of hours "cold trailing" through the woods. Once we got a good chorus of hound

125

music when the pack apparently surprised an old buck raccoon in a corn field. He immediately headed for high timber, then reversed his trail and lost his scent, and the dogs, in the water of a small creek.

Half an hour later we heard the faint sound of intermittent barking by the smallest of the dogs coming from the oak-maple woods high on one of the hills. Wild scrambling through tangled shrubbery and clinging vines finally brought us to the scene of action. We could see nothing in the dense canopy with our flashlights, so one hunter was elected to climb the oak tree.

Soon after he vanished from sight amidst a vast scraping of bark there came a complete silence. Someone shouted, "What is it, a skunk?" The somewhat disgruntled answer came back, "It's a danged porcupine. A big one. Grab the dogs."

We leashed the dogs, left the porcupine in its tree, and departed before we had a dequilling job on our hands. We never knew if the dog actually treed the porcupine or merely followed its trail to the base of the tree. It is even possible that the dog located the porcupine in the tree by the animal's pungent odor.

Deer antler gnawed by porcupines.

Porcupine den in winter near Oaknogan, Washington.

Many systems have been devised for handling porcupines for sexing, tagging, or other purposes. If you are in the woods without equipment, a forked stick can be used to hold the animal. The porcupine should be turned on its back, which may take a little doing. Then the crotch of the stick can be placed across the porcupine's chest while a partner steps on the animal's tail. The feet can be held apart with one's hands since the quills on the lower legs are small or nonexistent. Even then, gloves are recommended.

I have attempted to stop porcupines in their tracks by stepping on their tails. It works if you are careful, but there is always a chance of getting a leg full of quills. I have had a porcupine strike upward with its tail and leave several dozen quills imbedded a quarter-inch deep in the tough composition sole of my boot.

I prefer to stop them on the ground, if no other means is available, by holding the tail down with a heavy stick until with one hand I can grasp the hairs that project beyond the tip of the tail. Then the other gloved hand is slipped beneath the tail and the fingers closed with a slight backward movement. The tail is sturdy, and no harm is done if the porcupine is carried by it. The animal should be held away from one's legs since it can grasp a leg or ankle tightly with its fore paws.

An effective device for stopping porcupines on the ground is a cone made of chicken wire. The wire can be transported in a tight roll. When needed it can be quickly fashioned into a funnel with a lower

127

diameter of about two feet and a hole in the top, approximately eight inches across. When the animal is to be released, it can readily crawl out through the small end of the cone.

Porcupines can be transported nicely in small garbage cans or metal boxes. They can be transferred from one box to another by placing the containers gently on the ground with open sides facing one another. The animal should not be prodded or hurried. Generally it will make the move itself. A bamboo leaf rake is a good device for herding porcupines into a darkened box when you have the animals at home and have allowed them to graze dandelions on the lawn.

Getting a porcupine out of a tree can be a difficult and exciting procedure. A rope loop is not recommended since it may tighten and strangle the animal. A "come-along" stick has been recommended by Curtis and Kozicky. The device consists of a three-foot handle with a strong flexible wire attached at the lower end. The wire is threaded through a staple on the side of the handle at the bottom and through another staple half way up the stick. A toggle is made at the free end of the wire above the second staple. The loop that projects from the lower end of the handle can be tightened or loosened as the need arises. With this device the porcupine can be placed in a wire cone which then can be lowered to the ground with a rope.

Porcupine entering hole in the ground. Porcupines do not object to ground dens if not too wet.

Porcupines and Man

THE ANCESTRY OF THE PORCUPINE has been traced back to the Pleistocene age. This is a short time, when compared with the ant whose societies had already evolved at the time of the Eocene.

Sackett states: "Remains of a species, *Hystrix venustus*, have been found in the Pliocene of Nebraska, but it is probably more closely related to the Old World porcupine than to the American genus. There are also a few Tertiary South American genera, but nothing has been made out directly connecting them with the Erithizon genus."

In recent history, Coronado was one of the first of the American explorers to mention the porcupine. Undoubtedly he encountered many of them in his expedition through the Southwest in 1540.

Donald A. Spencer's fascinating study of porcupine population fluctuations in past centuries on Mesa Verde in southwestern Colorado has already been discussed. He was able to date feeding scars made on piñon pines as far back as the 145-year period of 1690–1835.

Man's effect on porcupines in America started with the Indians' hunting activities and with their use of the porcupine for food and for decorative purposes. The white man's effect undoubtedly began with the arrival of the first explorers on the northeastern coast of the continent. The effects were the result of direct action against the porcupine and of change in the animal's environment through clearing of timber and establishment of cultivated areas.

129

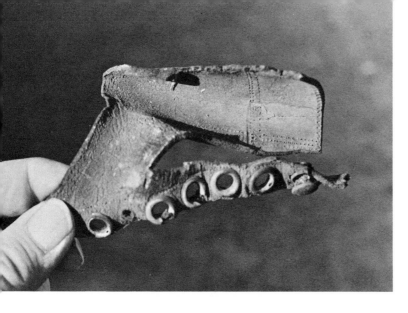

Porcupines like leather, especially old boots.

The greatest impact of man on porcupines has occurred since the beginning of the twentieth century. Most of the more than 400 references I have found on porcupines have been published since 1900. Much of this information indicates that white men and porcupines have come into real conflict only since man has attempted complete domination of the landscape for economic gain.

The Indians have long given recognition to the porcupine. The Ottawa and Cree Indians have woven porcupine quills over birch bark for generations in making knickknack boxes for jewelry and other trinkets. The Sioux decorated their moccasins with quills, and the Crow and other Indians used the polished quills for fancywork on buckskin shirts and elk skin robes. Quills also were used in making sewing baskets and war bonnets.

The Indians relished porcupine meat. Usually the animals were roasted whole. Thus they avoided the prickly job of skinning and at the same time prevented contamination of the meat with hair and soil.

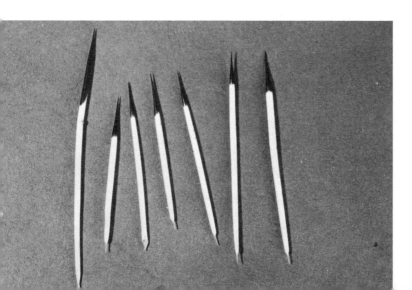

Quills.

Use by the Indians, however, did not decimate the populations of porcupines in the primitive forests of America.

The coming of the white man decidedly changed the world of the porcupine. The eastern forests were cleared for settlement. Cattle and other livestock introduced in the east at Jamestown and St. Augustine and in the Southwest gradually spread across the country. When they met on the plains of Kansas and Texas the conquest of the grazing

Porcupines never disturb their small associates in the woods—ground squirrels, chipmunks, rabbits, wood rats, mice, etc.

lands from deserts to mountains was well on the way to completion, with all its impacts on the native animals.

Later, the forests of the Lake States were depleted by timber cutters and fire. And in our own time the cutting of virgin timber on millions of acres in the West is proceeding with frightening tempo.

Now, in the latter half of the twentieth century, the nature of the land is being changed everywhere by people in cities, in towns, and on

The World of the Porcupine

roads; by grazing animals, cultivated crops, man-made lakes and reservoirs; by hunters, fishermen, recreationists, water users, and miners; and by a multitude of other factors, including poison sprays, pollutants, and pest-control activities carried on by individuals and government agencies. All these are making an impact on porcupine environment.

Conflicts invariably arise when wild animals use something that man wants for himself alone. The frequent response of man to something that interferes with his selfish desires is to get rid of the thing that interferes. For the porcupine, the penalty for eating a crop that the farmer grows or a tree the forester wants preserved is death. Since most of the predators have been killed or reduced to the vanishing point, man is now the porcupine's principal remaining enemy.

Porcupine country in the spruce-fir zone. Rocks for dens, meadows for summer food, trees for winter food.

Porcupine skull showing upper incisors.

Upper half of porcupine skull. The broad molars are adapted to masticating woody food.

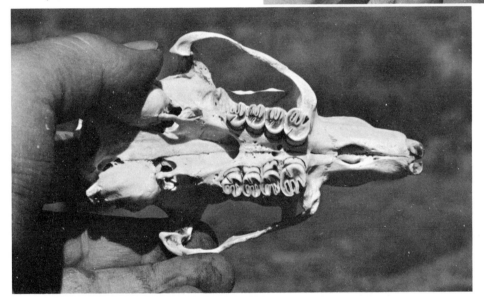

Taylor has suggested that porcupines in the Southwest increased their damage to trees because overgrazing by livestock destroyed their preferred herbage in summer. Unrestricted and excessive trapping and killing of natural predators, such as the fisher, the coyote, and the cougar, have brought about man-made eruptions of porcupines.

The almost cataclysmic destruction of some forest environments by timber cutting, followed by rapid secondary succession of herbaceous vegetation on millions of acres that have not been successfully refor-

Porcupine pellet shredded and greatly enlarged to show wood finely chewed by the animal's molars.

Porcupine pellets in winter are like little wood briquettes.

ested, has increased the environment favorable to porcupines and hence has increased the conflict between porcupines and men.

Not all published reports of damage by porcupines recommend extermination of these animals. A study of damage to white pines in Itasca Park and Forest states that many of the trees were salvagable even though they were killed by porcupines. The report says it would be unwise to eliminate porcupines in Itasca which is visited by thousands of people who are interested not alone in the trees, but in the wild creatures also.

Curtis and Kozicky after a five-year study of the eastern porcupine concluded that the damage wrought by porcupines in Hampshire County, Massachusetts, and Penobscot and Washington Counties, Maine, is infinitesimal in comparison with the volume of timber destroyed by fire, insects, fungi, and trail-blazing.

134

Porcupines and Man

Curtis, in another report, states: "The incorrect interpretation of the damage done in the stand by porcupines has undoubtedly contributed more to the prejudice against the animal than any other single factor. Although porcupines feed heavily and often kill individual trees, the effect upon the future development of the stand may be nil. . . . Killed trees that would otherwise be lost by natural competition should not be charged to the porcupine but only those final crop trees killed should be charged to him."

Because of encroachment of man on its habitat, the nation-wide range of the porcupine is shrinking. Few porcupines are seen now in the states on the southern border of their range in the middle states. Shapiro believes that they are probably now extirpated in Indiana, Ohio, Virginia, West Virginia, and Tennessee and that they are rare in New Jersey and some parts of Pennsylvania. In the West, and in Canada, porcupines are not as abundant as formerly owing to continued persecution in the forests.

It is widely accepted that the porcupine does considerable damage by its feeding habits in local areas. And on occasion it becomes a menace to livestock and dogs, and causes annoyance around cabins in the woods.

On the other hand, it does a certain amount of beneficial feeding on undesirable trees in mixed forest stands. But in general, it appears, from the more careful scientific studies, that the porcupine does not have a significant influence over large areas, either destructive or beneficial, in the modern forest "managed" by men.

Time was when the porcupine filled its useful niche in nature. It thinned out spots in the primeval forest so the sunlight could enter and the trees and herbs necessary for renewal of destroyed forests through natural succession could have a place to grow. Its thinning aided the growth of "all aged" instead of "single aged" stands and produced conditions conducive to mixtures of species that served all wild life in a profusion of plenty.

135

Ghost towns near timber line in Colorado are used for shelter by porcupines.

The porcupine once was a link in the food chain that allowed predators to maintain a more natural balance in the forest environment. It even helped the hares and the grouse by serving as a buffer food supply for the fisher, when that mortal enemy was abroad in the land.

The dried trunks of trees it girdled made homes for woodpeckers, and their homes made homes for other birds that helped control insect pests on living trees. And on occasion the porcupine even "controlled" an unwary hawk or great horned owl that misjudged the armor of its quills, and the porcupine thereby spared the life of a squirrel which then perhaps planted a few seeds that helped regenerate the forest.

Thus the porcupine is worthy of contemplation. It is unique. On that basis alone there is as much justification for its preservation as there is for preservation of the whooping crane, the California condor, the black-footed ferret, the ivory-billed woodpecker, or the golden eagle.

Porcupine country in northern Wisconsin. The animals wade in shallow water for lily pads.

Porcupine country in Michigan beech woods.

The porcupine is a symbol of our natural heritage, of a vanishing Eden, which is being transformed into a miasmatic jumble of buildings, freeways, polluted lakes, stinking rivers, and smoke-laden atmosphere. It is a symbol of the former quietness of forest and countryside that now is shattered by sonic booms and the roar of trucks and automobiles.

It is a symbol of a time when we did not put an economic value on all things and all creatures. It is an object worthy of understanding by men who will consider their own humble relationships with the natural world and their dependence on living creatures, both plant and animal.

137

Porcupine Subspecies

PORCUPINES BELONG TO the order Rodentia which includes such familiar animals as rats, mice, squirrels, gophers, and woodchucks. The family Erethizontidae includes the American porcupines which are represented by a single genus, *Erethizon*.

Mammalogists recognize seven subspecies of porcupines that live in northwestern Mexico, the United States, and Canada. The differences between these subspecies have been reviewed by R. M. Anderson and A. L. Rand in the *Canadian Journal of Research*.

The classification of subspecies and their geographic distributions also are described by Gerrett S. Miller and Remington Kellogg in *List of North American Recent Mammals* and by Raymond E. Hall and Keith R. Kelson in *The Mammals of North America*.

Erethizon dorsatum dorsatum. Canada porcupine. Range: This subspecies has the widest distribution of all the porcupines. It is found in much of the central and eastern parts of Canada and the United States. Its range extends from Nova Scotia to Alberta, Manitoba, Saskatchewan, and southern Yukon southward through the Northeastern States to West Virginia and westward to Wisconsin and Minnesota.

Erethizon dorsatum picinum. Labrador porcupine. Range: This porcupine is larger than *dorsatum* and is plain black without white-tipped hairs. It is common in Labrador and northeastern Quebec from

139

the Gulf of St. Lawrence north to the limit of trees. Its western limits are unknown.

Erethizon dorsatum myops. Alaska porcupine. Range: From the Yukon River in Alaska through Yukon and Northwest Territories to northern Alberta and British Columbia.

Erethizon dorsatum nigrescens. Dusky porcupine. Range: British Columbia and western Alberta in Canada and in the forested parts of Washington, exclusive of the Blue Mountains. They have been reported from the Olympic Peninsula.

Erethizon dorsatum bruneri. Nebraska porcupine. Range: Originally described from a specimen taken near Mitchell, Scotts Bluff County, Nebraska. It is believed to range from southern Saskatchewan southward to western Oklahoma and west to near Greeley, Weld County, Colorado.

Erethizon dorsatum epixanthum. California porcupine. Range: Throughout the western mountain states. It is common in Oregon, Washington, California, Nevada, Idaho, Utah, Montana, Wyoming, and Colorado. It also occurs in northeastern New Mexico. Anderson and Rand have reported it as an intergrade with *bruneri* in eastern Alberta and southwestern Saskatchewan, Canada.

Erethizon dorsatum couesi. Arizona porcupine. Range: The common porcupine in Arizona and New Mexico. It has been reported from the adjoining areas of southeastern Nevada, southwestern Colorado, southeastern Utah, and southwestern Texas. Also, it has been found in Sonora, Mexico, close to the Gulf of California.

Reading References

Alexander, R. "Billy the Prickly Pet." *Outing,* 73:299-300. March, 1919.

Anderson, R. M., and Rand, A. L. "Variation in the Porcupine (Genus *Erethizon*) in Canada." *Canadian Journal of Research,* Section D., 21:292-309. September, 1943.

Anonymous. "Birth to Porcupine Is Rare Blessed Event." *Science News Letter,* 41:345. May 30, 1942.

Anonymous. "Scrapping Acquaintance with the Dour and Prickly Porcupine." *Literary Digest,* 65:88. June 5, 1920.

Bailey, Vernon. *The Mammals and Life Zones of Oregon.* Washington, United States Department of Agriculture, 1936.

Banfield, A. W. F. "Distribution of the Barren Ground Grizzly Bear in Northern Canada," National Museum of Canada, Bulletin 166, Contrib. Zoology, 1958:47-59. 1958.

Batchelder, Charles Foster. "Notes on the Canada Porcupine." *Journal of Mammalogy,* 29:260-68. August, 1948.

Bauer, E. A. "Old Porky, Nobody's Pal." *Field and Stream,* 62:83. May, 1957.

Beck, R. "Don't Pet the Porcupines." *Outdoor Life,* 127:54-55. June, 1961.

Berry, W. D. "Aloysius, the Independent." *Audubon Magazine,* 56:212-15. September, 1954.

Blair, W. Frank, Blair, Albert P., Brokorb, Pierce, Cagle, Fred R., and Moore, George A. *Vertebrates of the United States.* New York, McGraw-Hill Book Company, Inc., 1957.

The World of the Porcupine

Branch of Predator and Rodent Control. *Vermont Porcupine Program*. United States Fish and Wildlife Service, Boston, 1959.

Bronson, Wilfrid S. "Heart's Rue and Self-defense." *Nature Magazine*, 36:512-18. December, 1943.

Brown, Pete. "State Guide to Varmint Hunting." *Sports Afield,* 154: 54-55. August, 1965.

Burell, A. E., and Ellis, R. "Mammals of the Ruby Mountain Region of Northeastern Nevada." *Journal of Mammalogy*, 15:12-44. 1934.

Burgdorfer, Willy. "Colorado Tick Fever. The Behavior of CTF Virus in the Porcupine." *Journal of Infectious Diseases*, 104:101-4. January-February, 1959.

Burroughs, John. "The Porcupine and His Quills." *Outing*, 45:247. November, 1904.

Burt, W. H., and Grossenheider, R. P. *A Field Guide to the Mammals*. Boston, Houghton Mifflin Company, 1952.

Cahalane, Victor H. *Mammals of North America*. New York, The Ronald Press Company, 1962.

Campbell, Sam. "Adventure with Porcupine." *American Forests*, 49:426-27; 463-64, September, 1943.

Carhart, Arthur Hawthorne. "Porky Spines." *Saturday Evening Post*, 199:78-80. October 16, 1926.

Chandler, Asa C. "The Genus Schizotaenia in Porcupines." *Journal of Parasitology*, 22:513. October, 1936.

Clyne, William D. "Room and Board." *Outdoor Life*, 114:4. December, 1954.

Cook, David B., and Hamilton, William J., Jr. "The Forest, the Fisher, and the Porcupine." *Journal of Forestry*, 55:719-22. October, 1957.

Coville, Frederick V. "Quills of a Porcupine." *National Geographic Magazine*, 23:25-31. January, 1912.

Cox, W. T. "Pine or Porcupine." *American Forestry*, 29:160-61. March, 1923.

Curtis, James D. "The Silvicultural Significance of the Porcupine." *Journal of Forestry*, 39:583-94. July, 1941.

Curtis, James D. "Appraisal of Porcupine Damage." *Journal of Wildlife Management*, 8:88-91. January, 1944.

Curtis, James D. "What They Say about Porky." *American Forests*, 52:474-75. October, 1946.

Reading References

Curtis, James D., and Kozicky, Edward L. "Observations on the Eastern Porcupine." *Journal of Mammalogy*, 25:137-46. May, 1944.

Curtis, James D., and Wilson, Alvin K. "Porcupine Feeding on Ponderosa Pine in Central Idaho." *Journal of Forestry*, 51:339-41. May, 1953.

Curtis, William. "Quill Pigs, Nature's Pincushion." *American Forests*, 57:16-17. August, 1951.

Dale, Bonnycastle, Jr. "Porky Lore." *Rod and Gun in Canada*, 39:15-16, 33-34. November, 1937.

Dalrymple, B. W. "Porcupine: Nature's Freak." *Coronet*, 32:64-66. June, 1952.

Devoe, A. "Porky—Question Mark of the Woods." *Country Gentleman*, 113:22, 40. November, 1943. (Also *Reader's Digest*, 43:69-71. December, 1943.)

Devoe, A. "Sex among the Porcupines." *American Mercury*, 72:603-6. May, 1951.

Dodge, Wendell, E. "Investigations Concerning the Repellency and Toxicity of Various Compounds for Control of Porcupine (*Erethizon D. Dorsatum,*" M.S. Thesis, University of Massachusetts. 1958.

Dodge, Wendell E. "An Effective Poison and Repellent for Porcupine Control." *Journal of Forestry*, 57:350-52. May, 1959.

East, B. "Not a Pig in a Poke." *Outdoor Life*, 118:8. July, 1956.

Eadie, W. Robert. *Animal Control in Field, Farm and Forest*. New York, The Macmillan Company, 1954.

Faulkner, C. E., and Dodge, W. E. "Control of the Porcupine in New England." *Journal of Forestry*, 60:36-37. January, 1962.

Finley, Bill. "Dinty Was a Porcupine." *Nature Magazine*, 20:181-82. October, 1932.

Flock, K. D. "The Porcupine—Friend or Foe?" *American Forests*, 40:308-10, 330. July, 1934.

Forest Service, United States Department of Agriculture. *Kinds of Injury Caused by Wildlife*. U. S. Forest Service Manual, Title 2600, Amendment 83. July, 1964.

Fosburgh, H. "Touchy Subject." *Field and Stream*, 65:39. June, 1960.

Freeman, R. S. "Notes on the Morphology and Life Cycle of the Genus *Monoecocestus* Beddard, 1914 (*cestoda: anoplocephalidae*) from the Porcupine." *Journal of Parasitology*, 35:605–12. December, 1949.

143

The World of the Porcupine

Freeman, R. S. "Biology and Life History of *Monoecocestus* Beddard, 1914 *(cestoda; anoplocephalidae)*." *Journal of Parasitology,* 38:111-29. April, 1952.

Fuller, R. "Fretful Porcupine." *Mentor,* 16:49. September, 1928.

Gabrielson, Ira N. "Notes on the Habits and Behavior of the Porcupine in Oregon." *Journal of Mammalogy,* 9:33-38. 1928.

Gabrielson, Ira N., and Horn, E. E. *Porcupine Control in the Western States.* U. S. Department of Agriculture, Leaflet, 60:1-8. 1930.

Geagan, B. "Word for Old Porky." *Nature Magazine,* 49:429-31. October, 1956.

Golley, Frank B. "Distribution of Porcupine in Upper Michigan." *Journal of Mammalogy,* 38:526-27. November, 1957.

Green, O. H. "Love Call of the Porcupine." *Nature Magazine,* 49:36. January, 1956.

Hall, E. Raymond. *American Weasels.* University of Kansas Publications, Museum of Natural History. Vol. 4. 1951.

Hall, E. Raymond, and Kelson, Keith R. *The Mammals of North America.* New York, The Ronald Press Company, 1959.

Hankinson, Hazel. "His Prickliness." *Better Homes and Gardens,* 9:61. November, 1930.

Highby, Paul R. "Studies in Filaroid Nematodes of the Porcupine and Snowshoe Hare in Minnesota." Ph.D. Thesis, University of Minnesota, 1942.

Highby, Paul R. *"Dipetalonema arbuta* N. SP. (Nematoda) from the Porcupine, *Erethizon dorsatum* (L)." *Journal of Parasitology,* 29:239-42. August, 1943.

Highby, Paul R. "Mosquito Vectors and Larval Development of *Dipetalonema arbuta* Highby (Nematoda) from the porcupine *Erethizon dorsatum." Journal of Parasitology,* 29:243-52. August, 1943.

Hulbert, W. D. "Pointers from a Porcupine Quill." *McClure's,* 15:312-24. August, 1900.

Hulbert, W. D. "Life of a Porcupine." *Current Literature,* 30:82-83. January, 1901.

Hunt, J. C. "BLM Aids Campaign Porcupine." *Our Public Lands,* 6:4-5. January, 1956.

Hunter, G. M. "Porcupines and the Damage They Do." Unpublished manuscript. District Two, U. S. Forest Service. Denver, pp. 1-18. 1917.

Reading References

Jaeger, E. "Fearless One." *Saint Nicholas*, 58:767. September, 1931.

Jellison, William L. "Parasites of Porcupines of the Genus *Erethizon* (Rodentia)." *Transactions of the American Microscopical Society*, 52:42-47. 1933.

Johnson, Mrs. M. "Spike and Mike." *Good Housekeeping*, 102:38-39. June, 1936.

Jonas, S. "Hound with Porcupine Quills." *American Veterinary Medical Association Journal*, 113:563. December, 1948.

Keller, L. Floyd. "Porcupines Killed and Eaten by a Coyote." *Journal of Mammalogy*, 16:232. 1935.

Knowlton, G. F., and Bruce, J. V. *Porcupines*. Utah Agricultural Experiment Station Circular 207 (1-2). 1954.

Kochersberger, Robert C. "Study to Determine Cranial and Dental Correlations with Age and Sex in the Canadian Porcupine, *Erethizon dorsatum dorsatum* (Linnaeus)." M.S. Thesis, University of Buffalo. 1950.

Krefting, L. W., Stoeckeler, J. H., Bradle, B. J., and Fitzwater, W. D. "Porcupine-Timber Relationships in the Lake States." *Journal of Forestry*, 60:325-30. May, 1962.

Kupree, L. "Who Saw the Sch'goon?" *Natural History*, 64:525-27. December, 1955.

Lathrop, G. A. "Porky Is a Clown." *Collier's*, 114:24. December 9, 1944.

Lawrence, J. E. "Nature's Paradoxical Dimwit; or the Beast with the Irritable Back." *American Mercury*, 77:133-34. November, 1953.

Lawrence, William H. "Porcupine Control: A Problem Analysis." *Weyerhaeuser Timber Company Forest Research Notes*. (Processed) July, 1957.

Loftin, H. "To Eat or Not." *Science News Letter*, 68:427. December 31, 1955.

Loveridge, A. "Hunting Porcupines with a Witch Doctor." *Natural History*, 56:404-7. November, 1947.

Ludeman, John. "Here's One Expert's Opinion on Porcupine Control." *Pest Control*, 22:26, 28, 30, 44. April, 1954.

MacGregor, A. E. "Late Fall and Winter Food of Foxes in Central Massachusetts." *Journal of Wildlife Management*, 6:221-24. 1942.

Manville, Richard H. "Notes on the Mammals of Mount Desert Island, Maine." *Journal of Mammalogy*, 23:391-98. November 14, 1942.

145

Marshak, R. R. "Injury of Gastro-intestinal Tract by Porcupine Quills." *American Veterinary Medical Association Journal*, 121:477. December, 1952.

Marshall, E. "Never Kill a Porcupine; Story." *American Mercury*, 90:22-25. December, 1920.

Marshall, W. H. "Radiotracking of Porcupines and Ruffed Grouse" (pp. 173-78), in Slater, L. R. *Bio-Telemetry. Interdisciplinary Conference.* New York, Pergamon Press, 1963.

Marshall, W. H., Gullion, Gordon W., and Schwab, Robert G. "Early Summer Activities of Porcupines as Determined by Radio-positioning Techniques." *Journal of Wildlife Management*, 26:75-79. January, 1962.

Mathiak, Harold A. "A Key to the Hairs of the Mammals of Southern Michigan." *Journal of Wildlife Management*, 2:251-68. October, 1938.

Merriam, C. H. *The Mammals of the Adirondack Region of Northeastern New York.* New York, L. S. Foster Press. First edition. 1884.

Milne, Lorus J., and Milne, Margery. "Prickly Problem." *New York Times Magazine*, pp. 97-98. March 15, 1959.

Mirand, Edwin A., and Shadle, Albert R. "Gross Anatomy of the Male Reproductive System of the Porcupine." *Journal of Mammalogy*, 34:210-20. May, 1953.

Mosteller, W., and Julian, F. "Porcupines in Relation to Wyoming Orchards." (In *Report 1917-1918,* pp 25-28, Wyoming State Board of Horticulture, Laramie. 1919.)

Munger, T. T. "Some Forest Problems of the Northwest, Particularly as They Relate to Sciences Other Than Forestry." *Northwest Science*, 2:38-44. 1928.

Musacchia, X. J., Wilber, C. G., and Gorski, T. W. "Hematological Studies on Mammals from Alaska." *Journal of Mammalogy*, 36:362-68. August, 1955.

Palmer, Ralph S. *The Mammal Guide.* Garden City, Doubleday & Company, 1954.

Payne, D. D., and O'Meara, D. C. "*Sarcoptes scabei* Infestation of a Porcupine." *Journal of Wildlife Management*, 22:321-22. July, 1958.

Reading References

Pearce, John. "Identifying Tooth Marks of Some Northeastern Animals on Forest Vegetation." *Transactions of the North American Wildlife Conference,* 3:690-94. 1938.

Perrin, E. O. "Our Friend the Porky." *Outing,* 70:645-50. August, 1917.

Perrota, Carmie Ann. "Fetal Membranes of the Canadian Porcupine, *Erethizon Dorsatum,* Linnaeus." Ph.D. Thesis, University of Wisconsin. 1956.

Pfeffer, Pierre. "Situation Actuelle de Quelques Animaux Menaces D'Indonesie." *La Terre et la Vie* (Paris) 105:128-45. 1958.

Po-Chedley, D. S. "A Method for Staining the Scales of Coarse Hairs." *Journal of Mammalogy,* 32:232. 1951.

Po-Chedley, Donald S., and Shadle, Albert R. "Pelage of the Porcupine, *Erethizon dorsatum dorsatum." Journal of Mammalogy,* 36:84-95. February, 1955.

Pulich, Warren M. "Some Porcupine Records for the Colorado River, Nevada." *Journal of Mammalogy,* 34:259-60. 1953.

Pulling, Albert Van S. "Porcupine Damage to Bighorn Sheep." *Journal of Wildlife Management,* 9:329. October, 1954.

Quick, Horace F. "Occurrence of Porcupine Quills in Carnivorous Mammals." *Journal of Mammalogy,* 34:256-59. May, 1953.

Reeks, W. A. "Notes on the Canada Porcupine in the Maritime Provinces." *Forestry Chronicle,* 18:182-87. December, 1942.

Reynolds, Hudson G. "Porcupine Behavior in the Desert-shrub Type of Arizona." *Journal of Mammalogy,* 38:418-19. August, 1957.

Roberts, G. D. "In Panoply of Spears." *Independent,* 54:1008-14. 1902.

Roberts, T. G. "The Canadian's Own Natural History Notes." *Canadian Magazine,* 85:38. January, 1936.

Rood, R. N. "Pokey." *Audubon Magazine,* 63:200-03. July, 1961.

Roth, Charles E. "Distribution of the Porcupine in Connecticut." *Journal of Mammalogy,* 38:133-35. February, 1957.

Rudolf, P. O. "Porcupines' Preferences in Pine Plantations." *Journal of Forestry,* 47:207-9. March, 1949.

Sackett, L. W. "The Canada Porcupine: A Study of the Learning Process." *Behavior Monographs.* Vol. 2, No. 2:1-84. Serial Number 7.

Savage, W. N. "Private Life of the Porcupine." *Science Digest,* 44:11-14. November, 1958.

The World of the Porcupine

Schoonmaker, W. J. "Porcupine Eats Water Lily Pads." *Journal of Mammalogy*, 11:84. February, 1930.

Schufeldt, R. W. "Woodchucks and Porcupines." *American Forestry*, 27:147-54. March, 1921.

Seton, E. T. "Porcupine at Home." *Country Life,* 17:415-16. February, 1910.

Seton, E. T. *Lives of Game Animals.* Boston, Charles T. Branford Company, 1953.

Shadle, Albert R. "Copulation in the Porcupine." *Journal of Wildlife Management*, 10:159-62. April, 1946.

Shadle, Albert R. "Feeding, Care and Handling of Captive Porcupines (*Erethizon*)." *Journal of Wildlife Management*, 31:411-16. 1950.

Shadle, Albert R. "Porcupine Spine Penetration." *Journal of Mammalogy*, 28:180-81. 1947.

Shadle, Albert R. "Natural Parturition of a Porcupine and First Reactions of a Porcupette." *Ohio Journal of Science*, 54:42-44. 1954.

Shadle, Albert R. "The Well-armed Porcupine." *Animal Kingdom*, 57:130-37. 1954.

Shadle, Albert R. "Effects of Porcupine Quills in Humans." *American Naturalist*, 89:47-49. January-February, 1955.

Shadle, Albert R., and Ploss, William R. "A Metal Restraining Tube for Animals." *Journal of Mammalogy*, 23:441-43. 1942.

Shadle, Albert R. and Po-Chedley, D. S. "Rate of Penetration of a Porcupine Spine." *Journal of Mammalogy*, 30:172-73. 1949.

Shadle, Albert R., Smelzer, Marilyn, and Metz, Margery. "Sex Reactions of Porcupine (*Erethizon d. dorsatum*) before and after Copulation." *Journal of Mammalogy*, 27:116-21. 1946.

Shapiro, Jacob. "Life History and Ecology of the Porcupine, *Erethizon d. dorsatum* L., on the Huntington Wildlife Forest Experiment Station, Newcomb, New York." M.S. Thesis, Syracuse University, 1947.

Shapiro, Jacob. "Ecological and Life History Notes of the Porcupine in the Adirondacks." *Journal of Mammalogy*, 30:247-57. 1949.

Shiras, George, 3rd. "A Flashlight Story of an Albino Porcupine and of a Cunning but Unfortunate Coon." *National Geographic Magazine*, 22:572-96. 1911.

Smith, G. S. "Thorny Assignment." *Audubon Magazine*, 62:180-83. July, 1960.

Reading References

Spalsbury, J. R. "Tim, a Pet Porcupine." *Audubon Magazine*, 59:114-16. May, 1957.

Spaulding P. *Investigations of the White Pine Blister Rust*. United States Department of Agriculture Bulletin 957, pp. 1-100. 1922.

Spencer, Donald A. "Porcupine Population Fluctuations in Past Centuries Revealed by Dendrochronology." *Journal of Applied Ecology*, 1:127-49. May, 1964.

Spencer, Donald A. *The Porcupine as a Factor in Regeneration of Hurricane Areas*. Fox Forest Notes, No. 29. New Hampshire Forestry and Recreation Department. 1941

Spencer, Donald A. "A Forest Mammal Moves to the Farm—the Porcupine." *Transactions of the North American Wildlife Conference*, 11:195-99. 1946.

Spencer, Donald A. "An Electric Fence for Use in Checking Porcupine and Other Mammalian Crop Depredations." *Journal of Wildlife Management*, 12:110-11. 1948.

Spencer, Donald A. *The Porcupine: Its Economic Status and Control*. United States Department of the Interior, Fish and Wildlife Service, Wildlife Leaflet 328. May, 1950.

Spencer, Donald A. "Porcupines, Rambling Pincushions." *National Geographic Magazine*, 98:247-64. August, 1950.

Sperry, G. "Those Pesky Porcupines." *American Cattle Producer*, 36:19. May, 1955.

Squier, E. L. "Friends of a Quill." *Good Housekeeping*, 75:52-54. December, 1922.

Stone, J. Herbert. "Porcupine Damage to Trees Serious in Northwest." *Journal of Forestry*, 50:891. November, 1952.

Struthers, Parke H. "Breeding Habits of the Canadian Porcupine (*Erethizon dorsatum*)." *Journal of Mammalogy*, 9:300-08. 1928.

Struthers, Parke H. "Aortic Arches and Their Derivatives in the Embryo Porcupine *Erethizon dorsatus*." *Journal of Morphology*, 50:361-92. December, 1930.

Swena, Richard, and Ashley, Laurence M. *Osteology of the Common Porcupine Erethizon dorsatum*. Publications of the Department of Biology. Science and Biological Station, Walla Walla College, 18:1-26. December, 1956.

Taft, R. E. "Conifers Curse." *American Forestry*, 22:283-84. May, 1916.

149

Taylor, Walter P. "Four Thousand Dollar Dog." *American Forests*, 34:151-53. March, 1928.

Taylor, Walter P. *Ecology and Life History of the Porcupine (Erethizon epixanthum) as Related to the Forests of Arizona and the Southwestern United States.* University of Arizona Bulletin VI (Biological Science Bulletin 3). July, 1935.

Thone, F. "Not Necessarily a Nuisance." *Science News Letter*, 40:222. October 4, 1941.

Trippensee, R. E. *Wildlife Management.* New York, McGraw-Hill Book Company, Inc., 1953.

Tyron, C. A., Jr. "Behavior and Post-natal Development of a Porcupine." *Journal of Wildlife Management*, 11:282-83. July, 1947.

VanDeusen, James L., and Myers, Clifford A. "Porcupine Damage in Immature Stands of Ponderosa Pine in the Black Hills." *Journal of Forestry*, 60:811-13. November, 1962.

Walker, Ernest P., Warnick, Florence, Lange, Kenneth I., Uible, Howard E., Hamlet, Sybil E., Davis, Mary A., and Wright, Patricia F. *Mammals of the World.* 3 vols., Baltimore, The Johns Hopkins Press, 1964.

Warren, Edward Royal. *The Mammals of Colorado.* Norman, University of Oklahoma Press, 1941.

Wood, A. S. "Snowball in a Spruce; Albino Porcupine." *Nature Magazine*, 50:136. March, 1957.

Wright, Bruce S. "Some Forest Wildlife Problems in New Brunswick." *Forestry Chronicle*, 27:330-34. December, 1951.

Index

Index

Index